THE JOURNEY INTO WHOLENESS

Daphne
Publications

THE JOURNEY INTO WHOLENESS

A Jungian Guide to Discovering the Meaning of Your Life's Path

BUD HARRIS, PHD

DAPHNE PUBLICATIONS • ASHEVILLE, NORTH CAROLINA

THE JOURNEY INTO WHOLENESS:
A JUNGIAN GUIDE TO DISCOVERING THE MEANING OF YOUR LIFE'S PATH
COPYRIGHT © 2020 BY BUD HARRIS, PHD

DAPHNE PUBLICATIONS, AN IMPRINT OF SPES, INC.

Harris, Clifton T. Bud
The journey into wholeness: a Jungian guide to discovering the meaning of your life's path / Bud Harris

ISBN 978-0-578-62382-5 Non-fiction
1. Psychology 2. Jungian Psychology 3. Spirituality

Library of Congress Control Number: 2016908974
Spes, Inc, Asheville, NC

Interior Layout by Susan Yost

I have frequently seen people become neurotic when they content themselves with inadequate or wrong answers to the questions of life. They seek position, marriage, reputation, outward success or money, and remain unhappy and neurotic even when they have attained what they were seeking. Such people are usually confined within too narrow a spiritual horizon. Their life has not sufficient meaning. If they are enabled to develop more spacious personalities, the neurosis generally disappears. For that reason the idea of development was always of the highest importance to me.

– C.G. JUNG

The meaning of 'whole' or 'wholeness' is to make holy or to heal. The descent into the depths will bring healing. It is the way to the total being, to the treasure which suffering mankind is forever seeking, which is hidden in the place guarded by terrible danger.

– C.G. JUNG

Author's Note:

All stories, dialogues, and dreams in this book, except those I specifically designate as being my own, reflect material people have shared with me. To protect the privacy of those people, I have carefully altered anything that might disclose the identity of particular individuals or permit the identification of actual relationships or circumstances. Any similarity between the people and situations I have used for illustration and actual people or situations is unintended and purely coincidental.

Bud Harris, PhD
Asheville, North Carolina

Contents

PART TWO—THE TRUE GOLD

Introduction

Whenever I can, before starting my workday as a Jungian analyst, I like to spend some quiet time mulling over my leftover thoughts and dreams from the preceding day and evening. This book began as a series of such reflections.

I was thinking of Ed Robbins, the last analysand I had seen the day before. Ed was forty-four years old, married, and the father of three children. A year before, he had been diagnosed with a malignant tumor. Normal cancer treatment called for an invasive surgical procedure that would have left him horribly disfigured, physically handicapped, and unable to continue in his profession. Further, the surgery didn't—and couldn't—guarantee a cure.

Ed decided, after a period of consuming study and consultations, to pursue an alternative course of treatment. He also chose to pursue Jungian analysis as he sought a deeper understanding of himself and the process he and his family were going through.

The previous evening Ed had come into his session, sat down, and exclaimed, "I feel so full of life that I'm about to explode! I'm so full of joy and pain. I could laugh or cry. To be honest with you," he continued, "it's driving me a little crazy. I could start crying and wouldn't know whether they were tears of pain or joy."

Ed and his family found that their experience had taken a surprising turn. They were learning to *live*—in one of the hardest possible ways—and through their ordeal they were discovering dimensions of themselves and of life, dimensions of meaning and vitality they could not have imagined previously. Of course, they were still confused, deeply concerned, and scared. Paradoxically, his cancer seemed to have emerged as an inner teacher that was instructing Ed and his family on the importance of a fuller way of life than they had been leading.

As I write this, it's too early to tell if his condition is really improving, but what we do know is that each day has become a blessing for them.

My analytic sessions with Ed often seem to rumble around in my psyche for days, as do sessions with many others, especially those who are involved with illness. I am almost forced to meditate on the depth and complexity of my sessions with these people. Their *diseases* are teaching me as much as anything else. In each case I am repeatedly impressed with how easily, in the course of life's daily mechanics, they—and all of us—seem to lose our sense of the mystery of life. The climate of fantasy and wonder that exists in the natural world and in our imaginations is lost among jobs, families, responsibilities, and the problems of everyday living. We seem almost to reach a point where only an event that inspires great dread can interrupt our hectic pace and break through conventional barriers to return us to this mystery—a mystery we cannot control, despite our rational mind and scientific methodologies. It is a mystery we seek to deny on a daily basis.

Ed's wife said his diagnosis hit their family like a bolt out of the blue. In a mythological sense, this term is an apt one, for lightning has always symbolized the voice of a god or God, intruding upon our lives. Such an intrusion is a call to greater consciousness and a summons to us as human beings to renew our lives and increase our awareness. Such bolts are usually followed by a roll of thunder that underlines the dread of this imperative, as well as the consequences that would confront us should we fail to respond to it.

Intrusive dread quickly reminds us how easily ordinary outer events can be enfolded in profound moments, as a larger sense of life breaks through our awareness. Suddenly, the great unknown has presented itself to us personally, with a transparency that reveals the potential darkness that surrounds us. These events remind us of our solitariness and our isolation, for who may feel more

alone than someone entering an MRI tunnel, having a heart cathe-
ter, or lying down on the treatment platform for radiation therapy?
Or should we ask, "Who is more aware of their reality?"

These kinds of situations return our attention to the fact that
we live in, and our lives reflect, two patterns. One seems to belong
to us—we own it through our personal experiences. And one seems
to belong to life itself. As we develop a more profound sense of conscious awareness, we can begin to recognize our personal pattern.
And if we pursue even greater consciousness, we will be able to
see through that personal pattern and perceive the structure of the
other pattern—*life's* pattern, or patterns—which supports us and is
likewise being lived through us.

The pattern that belongs to life represents the general
developmental path of all people. In Jungian psychology, we
call this pattern and its various elements *archetypal*. It is general
to all human beings and is mirrored in the overall story of
human development. These collective, archetypal patterns of
human development are also reflected in myths, fairy tales, and
legends, and they are often shown to us individually in dreams,
fantasies, and other creative expressions. In addition, human
history frequently seems to demonstrate its own psychological
development, to the extent that it reflects characteristics and
stages similar to those in personal development. Thinking of
the developmental patterns as a sort of elemental blueprint
that resides in the collective unconscious may be helpful. The
collective unconscious is the layer in our psyche that structures
our mental and physical activities and generally operates beneath
the level of our normal conscious functioning.

Living authentically means discovering our way in life through
our own experience and the self-knowledge that can result from ex-
amining this experience. It doesn't mean trying to learn the crucial
answers to life's questions from some dogmatic or abstract framework. Unfortunately, most of the developmental maps in traditional psychology and religion are too general, too abstract, and
too focused on carving us into a particular form or bringing us to a

predefined state to be of much help as we seek to fulfill a pattern of personal authenticity—the quest of the individual soul.

Each of us is a unique creation who develops through experiences particular to us, though we are affected by the context into which we are born. A knowledge of the elemental, archetypal patterns can amplify and inform our life and the way we experience it, as well as help us better define our struggles, wounds, and paths to healing. To this end, I will call on these patterns through citing stories, myths, case studies, and dreams to help us understand how we develop through our experiences and how these experiences relate to the elemental blueprint.

It might be helpful to look at these patterns in another way. We can imagine that life is like a river that channels and supports our personal experiences. Beneath this river lies another river that channels and supports the flow of all life. A river beneath a river— the first river representing our personal pattern and the second one representing the archetypal patterns in the collective unconscious. When we are cut off from the deeper river, whether we know it or not, we are cut off from the source of life. We will dry up and burn out. And we will be prisoners of a mind-set that rests on the effects of our childhood and the values of society. If we can rediscover our deeper and natural part, we can find the nourishment necessary to reconstruct ourselves and live in an authentic way. A knowing of the soul, the true experience of life and wholeness, comes from an awareness of the deeper pattern, the river of all life beneath the river of our life.

Both types of patterns—the personal and the archetypal—are embedded in each other, as both require life to exist. We are the carriers of that life and its experiences. Many of the conflicts and paradoxes we encounter are the result of our being stuck (with or without awareness of the fact) either in our personal pattern or between the two patterns, as we will see later in this book. If we are thoughtful, the dread that comes from the lightning bolts of life can return us to our longing for understanding, to a wondering about the before and after in our lives as well as about the now.

As a result of this understanding, we may find a better focus as we watch our step *today* and uncover issues within us that are unlived and unfinished.

We may also discover that there is a pattern of creation longing to be fulfilled within each of us as well as in life in general. Finding that pattern and working toward its fulfillment is what Jungians call the *individuation* process. By recognizing and understanding our human journey from birth to death, we can acknowledge the mileposts we all encounter in the general pattern. As we study this process, we can look steadily at our own patterns, our lives, as a journey toward wholeness and completion.

Because I am writing as a Jungian analyst and in the context of Jungian psychology (a context I will explain in the opening of Chapter 1, in "The Spirit of Individuation"), I want first to mention a few things about the practice of Jungian analysis. We who take a Jungian perspective think of one's imagination as the field where, in waking life, the conscious and unconscious minds meet in creative endeavors. Within this imaginative field, one may often dialogue with figures from dreams and other psychological components of the personality. (In several places in the manuscript I am in dialogue with the inner feminine figure within myself known, in Jungian language, as my anima, my inner *She*.[1]) We may also dialogue with our illnesses, emotions, attitudes, and so on. To name and identify an inner attribute changes our relationship to it. As a result of such changes, we become more discerning and mature psychologically and have a more objective connection to these parts of ourselves. Thus, they often lose their power to possess our consciousness and dominate our behavior. The work between the analyst and analysand is founded upon dialogues in this creative field.

Sam Keen, the well-known author in religion and psychology, used a similar process in developing one of his books. He notes that

---

1   "Anima" is the Jungian term for the eternal or archetypal image of a woman carried within a man's psychology and the feminine nature of his unconscious. For a woman, it is the "animus" who personifies the image of her masculine nature. (For a brief amplification of this concept, see footnote 5, Chapter 2.)

such dialogue "…records many of the conversations that take place between the voting members of the commonwealth that is Sam Keen."[2] He goes on to give clear examples of his method of dialoguing with inner parts of himself. If you are interested in this process, I recommend his book as an excellent model for beginning. You will also see this technique illustrated in many of the following chapters, which will reflect the importance of developing and "I and thou" relationship within ourselves. A number of times as I write about our personal journey, I will use the analogy of boundary crossings. This analogy refers to those times in our development when we must, whether we want to or not, outgrow the limits of our current personality and self-image in order to continue our individuation. If our personal pattern bogs down, the greater pattern of life will often supply the needed impetus, perhaps a bolt from the blue, to get us moving. Big or small, one of these boundary crossings is always before us—sometimes nearby, sometimes far away.

Throughout the book, I will mention *eros* and its many levels of complexity. Although eros has, historically, had various meanings, it originally symbolized profound mythological power. In the early Greek creation story, Eros was born at the beginning of time out of chaos and brought together the sky god and the earth mother. Eros then presided over all generativity and exemplified the power that fueled the cycle of life, death, and renewal. I will follow this earlier notion of meaning for the word "eros," and use it to represent the life force *per se* on all levels. It also includes love on all levels: erotic, sexual, romantic, brotherly, spiritual, and so on.

On the instinctual level, eros acts to continue the species. It represents the generative force that brings all living things to life and gives them the imperative to grow. It represents the imperative for us as human beings to fulfill the pattern within ourselves not only for physical development but for spiritual and psychological development as well. In the Jungian tradition, I will refer to this aspect of eros as *individuating eros*. This imperative to grow

---

2   Sam Keen, *To a Dancing God: Notes of a Spiritual Traveler* (San Francisco: Harper, 1970). See the discussion on pages 106-140.

continues to manifest itself even when we are wounded or blocked, most noticeably in emotional and physical symptoms of disease.

Individuating eros, as the general imperative to grow, is what plunges us into relationships—those within ourselves, with other people, and with society—that will cause us either to continue to differentiate and evolve or to wither and die. This aspect of eros thus underlines another basic aspect of life, which is that for full development, we all need each other. It represents the inner force that pressures us to develop qualities of relatedness, which stand for life and bring life to a sense of wholeness and completion until, in the words of the dying king in Verdi's opera, "A Masked Ball," "Love conquers death!" This is the spirit in which I will use the term *individuating eros*.

In the Judeo-Christian tradition, we find that in the beginning was the "Word," perhaps implying that order and form should dominate creativity. Eros, the urge to continual and eternal creativity, was imaged in the Garden of Eden as a *snake*. This imaging sets up the dynamic tension between order and creativity, between structure and renewal, that has evolved in Western civilization. The snake is a highly significant personal symbol of this forgotten god and a friend to the individuation process. The symbolic snake in the Garden of Eden represents the urge to grow that causes us to commit the necessary sin against our inner and outer conventions. This sin will lead us into sufficient conflict to force us to cross the boundary of our current development. *Individuating eros* is the primal force in life, symbolized by the snake and arising from our unconscious, which upsets order in the compelling quest for further development.

The purpose of this book is simply to show how the concepts I am discussing work in life, how we experience them, and how we can understand them better. They exist in all the stages of our development, as I try to illustrate by moving my discussion from birth until death.

As our life begins, we must develop a personality from the unconscious conditions of childhood that will enable us to live effectively in society. In the second half of life, we must seek a more personal relationship with the center of ourselves and life, in order for our life to become an authentic personal expression of who we are and who we are meant to be. Thus, in Part One, I have tried to illustrate the context of development that leads us in the direction that evolves in Part Two. This evolution seems to begin with a digression, a general feeling of uneasiness and disturbance, perhaps even a crisis. But, as is frequently the case, we discover that such a digression is heralding a turning point in our growth, as digressions often do.

As the book passes into Part Two, I hope you will find our relationship becoming deeper and more personal.

In addition, I try to illustrate that there is an "other," a *Self*, orchestrating our lives and trying to help us grow by using the creative spirit of life—eros—again and again in bringing us face-to-face with life and ourselves. I also want to show that our struggles have meaning, and that eros and intensity are crucial to any true life.

Finally, I seek to show that true peace, the feeling of being at home in life, lies at the symbolic intersection of the cross, where contradictions—the paradoxical components of life's struggles—converge. Psychologically, the structure of the cross represents the ways by which we are pulled in opposite directions—vertically and horizontally—until, paradoxically, this point moves from one at the center of suffering and death to one of transformation and new life. This movement depends on our willingness to fully engage life, accept the pain of growth, and follow the inward quest for self-knowledge. In this manner, we absorb our pain and transform it into creativity. This process is illustrated in a dream in the closing pages where in the dreamer learns that the contradictions of his life must come together and that he must learn to experience them, both within and without, as his own.

I hope this book will help you know and understand yourself better. I believe your reflections on it will bring you a deeper awareness of your embeddedness in life and how experiencing this relationship, this unity, can constantly challenge and renew you. Consciously observing your life's journey in this new context can imbue you with a love of life and a sense of hope that can never be justified by literal perceptions and superficial explanations of life. Perhaps you will also find that peace is the result of finding your heart and wholeness in the midst of living your journey.

PART ONE

THE COMMON GOLD

Individuation means becoming a single homogeneous being, and, insofar as "individuality" embraces our innermost, last, and incomparable uniqueness, it also implies becoming one's own self. We could therefore translate individuation as "coming to selfhood" or "self-realization."

...Individuation does not shut one out from the world, but gathers the world to oneself.

– C.G. JUNG, *MEMORIES, DREAMS, REFLECTIONS*, PP. 395-396

The remnants of the child-soul in the adult are his best and worst qualities; at all events they are the mysterious spiritus rector *of our weightiest deeds and of our individual destinies, whether we are conscious of it or not...behind every individual father there stands the primordial image of the Father, and behind the fleeting personal mother the magical figure of the Magna Mater.*

– C.G. JUNG, *C.W.*, VOL. 20, PAR. 97

Chapter 1

A LIFE OF OUR OWN

The Spirit of Individuation

The underlying principle of Jungian psychology is that our life story, if it is truly lived, brings about the realization of our inner and often unconscious potentials. From this perspective, we see that the goal of life is to achieve wholeness of the personality by bringing to light and integrating into our consciousness certain aspects of our nature that are presently unconscious. In more practical terms, it means we are called to discover and fulfill the inherent pattern for development that lies within us. This process results in the unfolding of the totality of our personality in both the inner and the outer worlds.

A fulfilling life is one that is continually bringing our inner patterns into conscious expression and completion. There are few traditional textbooks, scientific systems, or religious techniques that can do any more than give us a little help along our way as we seek the kind of self-knowledge that leads to individuation. The knowledge required for this task can only come through increased conscious awareness based on our experience in living and our relationship to our interior life.

Self-understanding and self-realization are key concepts in Jungian psychology, but they are not simply intellectual terms. They must be married to values of the heart. Originally, they emanated from the "heart of the physician" in Dr. Jung, who felt great compassion for people's suffering and wanted to help them find healing. As Jung grew into his later years, it is clear that his heart expanded into a deep concern for the problems and the future of humanity and culture.

In Jung's view, the unconscious itself wishes to be understood and wishes to help both individuals and culture heal and grow. In other words, it wishes to be manifested and lived. Of course, Dr. Jung was not naïve. He realized that dangerous things also lurk within us, and, as a result, he felt that the work of individuation must be done carefully and that it requires a strong, well-developed personality. Such a personality, with a sense of ethics and a secure rootedness in the outer world, is the foundation of the second half of an individual's development.

Jung often compared the development of our personality to the course of the sun during the day. With birth—dawn in his allegory—our consciousness begins to shine and marks the beginning of our personality development. Our early development is characterized by the push for identity, action, achievement, and external relationships. This push requires a large amount of emotional energy and the eventual sacrifice of our childhood dependency. Hopefully, this effort will culminate in a strong personality and a place in society as we fulfill the psychological tasks from late adolescence to early adulthood and beyond. When we reach midlife, our "sun" is at its zenith, in its position of greatest strength. At this point the sun begins to set, losing its position of strength as it follows nature's course. Similarly, at that midlife point, we must begin releasing our focus on our identity and achievement, redirecting our energy toward becoming *whole*.

The first step in this process is to start reclaiming parts of ourselves that were lost in our struggle to reach that zenith. Of course, we have a choice at this point. We can choose to resist nature, the greater pattern of life, and protect what we have achieved. But nature, in such a case, will generally escalate the unconscious assaults against our personality in the form of neurosis, addictions, and illnesses.

In a general sense, Jungian psychology considers the unconscious to be the psychic counterpart of the world of nature. The taproot of our inner "nature" is rooted in the collective unconscious, which contains the psychic energy centers and patterns that animate us. These natural forces are common to everyone. Often, they are so powerful that they have a numinous quality. As a result, they have been projected outward in the images of gods, goddesses, and other spiritual symbols throughout history.

Another goal of our later life is to face the inevitability of death, as nature decrees that our allegorical sun must also set. The search for wholeness and the completion of our personal pattern is, in Jung's mind, our preparation for death and eternity. As our energy shifts to this inner search, we still have to contend with our outer life and face its obligations. But we must change our focus from the bright daylight of external development to the softer, more diffused light of our inner world. This new focus can lead to an inner rootedness, a relationship with the transcendent, and a concern for culture. As this process proceeds, our personality will be broadened, our life will be deepened, and our experiences will approach an unexpected sense of unity within themselves.

In summary, we see that the Jungian perspective divides the development of the personality into two fundamental periods. The first is from birth to psychological midlife, commonly referred to as "the first half of life." The second is from psychological midlife to death, and is commonly referred to as "the second half of life."

During the first half of life, our basic developmental task is to differentiate a personality as we grow out of childhood. That personality should be strong enough to find a place and to form relationships in the external world of societal life. It should be able to function effectively there, according to the common standards, aims, and goals of that world. In symbolic terms, this achievement is referred to in Jungian psychology as finding the *common gold*.

Generally, once this task is completed, we begin feeling lost— as though somehow, in achieving our place in life, we have lost ourselves. That is, we do so if we are alert enough to let that much self-awareness through our defenses. If we don't or can't, we will develop some other attention-getting type of symptom, usually expressed in the form of an emotional or physical dis-ease. In either case, our primary task in the second half of life is to come into relationship with our unconscious and the center of our being—our *Self*—by finding our soul and the meaning of our life. In this way, we discover the *true gold*, the symbol of the illuminated soul.

The Jungian analyst must take nature as his or her guide. What we do in analytic sessions is not so much therapy as it is furthering the development of the creative seed inherent in the analysand and nurturing that development. This process often includes going backward in a person's life—especially family life—and helping the person create a friendly inner background in which his or her reconstruction can begin.

Once the corner is turned from the first half of life to the second, one discovers that a lifestyle that looks good and works (no matter how well) isn't sufficient to provide the true gold of fulfillment. This realization alone is enough to give us an idea of how difficult the work of individuation can be.

During this turning point in personal growth, suffering evolves to a higher level. In this context, suffering comes to mean expending "blood, sweat, and tears" with religious devotion in the effort to discover the true gold of our nature. It represents the courage to depart from conventional wisdom, ambition, pleasures, comforts, pride, and values in favor of following the creative voice within us. There are many possible wrong turns and no guarantees of success in this journey. But if we are successful, genuine self-realization rewards us by giving birth to a deeper experience of love, compassion, and joy in our lives.

Another of Jung's cardinal concepts is that of the *Self*. For Jung, the Self is the central archetype of order within the personality, and it also represents the totality of the personality as well as its center. The Self embraces both the conscious and unconscious elements in our psyche. However, as an archetype, it is nevertheless located in the unconscious. Dr. Jung noted that "the Self is our life's goal, for it is the completest expression of the fateful combination we call individuality."[1] In simple language, we can say, as Jung did, that the Self is the image of God within us. It is our center and it also represents the pattern of all we are meant to be. The energy of this central point issues a psychological imperative to us to "become what we are," just as biology compels us to assume the form of a human being. In Jungian psychology, our ego is regarded as the center of our conscious personality, while the Self is the center of our whole personality and the carrier of our potential. Often these two centers may be on contradictory paths, thereby causing us a lot of conflict.

For example, our ego may be seeking material success, security, and conventional satisfaction, while our Self is more interested in the creative fulfillment of our life. The Self also requires us not simply to be, but also to *become*. As you may recognize, this requirement is the foundation of the spiritual principle that underlies Western religious thought and doesn't allow us to retire from life.

Once we have begun our individuation process, we come into an increasingly conscious relationship with the Self. As this relationship deepens, we start to realize that a hidden hand seems to be—and to have been—holding onto, guiding, and supporting us throughout our life. In different parts of this book, I refer to this guiding aspect of the Self variously as the *hidden teacher*, the *inner teacher*, or the *hidden healer*. When we are truly in touch with this aspect of ourselves, no experience (regardless of how devastating) is meaningless or without value: each contributes to the true gold.

The Paradox of Peace

Peace is a dominant issue as we look into the health needs of today's world. The management of stress and the practice of techniques that bring inner calmness are included in many alternative forms of medicine and are generally being accepted by mainstream medical practitioners. Peace is one state that means something to practically

---

1   C.G. Jung, *Memories, Dreams, Reflections*, ed. A. Jaffé, trans. Richard and Clara Winston (New York: Random House, 1973), 398.

everyone, as well as seeming vitally important to our health. It is desired by people everywhere—rich and poor, old and young. And the search for it is as old as humanity.

The greatest epic stories, almost as old as our ability to speak, are about such searches—travels through strange lands in search of home, the quest for a secure sense of peace both within and without. But this perpetual longing, like the frantic tempo of our stressful lives, is proof that we haven't found it.

Even though our yearning for peace seems eternal, most ancient pantheons had no principal god or goddess of peace. The early Greeks simply viewed peace as the opposite of war, and personified the absence of external conflict as the goddess Eirene, who had a small cult and no mythology. Death for these ancient Greeks brought no peace either, for death meant eternally being in a sense of nothingness, existing as shades, images with no substance, in the underworld.

Eastern religions take an opposite, less aggressive approach than the West's emphasis on becoming, promising us peace if we can empty ourselves. But this is not an easy task, and even the great Buddha lived a life of inner struggle, leading to his statement that all life is sorrowful. For those living a practical life, the history of the East hasn't been any more peaceful than that of the West.

Christ is often spoken of as the "Prince of Peace" and Christians throughout the world offer each other Christ's peace on Sunday. But the life of Christ, too, was filled with passionate suffering, torment, and vilification from many of the people around him. Those who truly undertake the Christian's journey likewise find their lives filled with passion and suffering. Further, the mystic way in the Western traditions—seeking union with God or the higher self—is no peaceful experience either, and is described as "seeking the flame." When the Holy Spirit descended at Pentecost, it came as tongues of flame. It was not carried down by doves.

Peace is a mystery we continually misunderstand. Frequently we deny life and vitality, wrecking our development while desperately trying to grasp a hollow version of peace, or at least create the illusion that we have it. Every therapist I know will simply shake his or her head if you ask how many people have watched marriages disintegrate beyond repair rather than challenge their illusion of peace. However, the force of peace and the longing for peace continues to draw all humanity toward an unknown destiny. Acknowledging this, I will present my reflections on peace and its place in our patterns of life throughout the upcoming pages.

As we are trained and indoctrinated by our institutions, society teaches us that maturity means a resolution of contraries. We are in control; we know what we are doing and where we are going. We also maintain a positive attitude and, if we are psychologically minded, we focus on becoming self-actualized. One of the most painful aspects of individuation is learning that these types of perspectives are simply illusions. Life is full of contradictions we can't control; in fact, they are integral to it. They are not here by accident, and they are not due to our inept or dysfunctional behavior.

The journey of individuation sharpens and magnifies our awareness of these contradictions. The truths we discover as we search for the true gold highlight the untruths we accepted when we were pursuing the common gold. If we are genuinely living, we become increasingly aware of life's contradictions because we encounter so many of them. Instead of fleeing from their tension or simplifying them by being blind to one or more of their aspects, we must allow them into the center of our existence. As we accept them, we have begun to love life's questions. Conflicts are transformed into paradoxes and become the pathway to a larger personality and the expression of the deeper truth of ourselves that will lead to a life larger than we could have previously imagined.

In this process, we don't abandon our ability to think and make judgments; in fact, we refine these abilities. Jung referred to this process as "holding the tension of the opposites." Becoming whole means being committed to holding these tensions consciously, fully, and, when necessary, painfully. Then, as our Self plunges us into the paradox at its center, we will find our lives transformed and shifted to a new position, closer to that which expresses our

Self and full of renewed vitality. Jung termed this particular process the "transcendent function." By the time we realize the answer to one of our predicaments, we will understand that it came from our having lived it and reflected upon it.

Jung considered paradox (something contrary to expectation or general opinion, or which is seemingly opposed to common sense and yet appears to be true) to be the expression of the tension of opposites, especially those between the conscious and unconscious elements of our psyche. William Blake noted, "Without Contraries there is no progression. Attraction and Repulsion, Reason and Energy, Love and Hate, are necessary to Human existence."[2] From this perspective, opposites do not truly express duality, for they are connected. They are opposite ends on a continuum of experience, related and joined. We would like to bring them into our personality, as is needed for wholeness, without severing them from each other or depriving them of their vital intensity.

Most of us, unfortunately, aren't aware of this process. We are too busy chasing the common gold and shallow illusions of peace.

Reflection, Insight and Understanding

In the venerable mythology of northern Europe, we find a mythic pattern that encompasses consciousness, fate, and wisdom. In his quest for wisdom, Odin, the "All-Father" god, was required to visit the well of the wizened hag, Mirmir. In exchange for his being able to drink from the well and gain a knowledge of fate and wisdom, the hag required an eye from him, which he surrendered to her. In this ancient tale, his remaining eye was known thereafter as the sun. This solar eye represents solar consciousness (the symbol for rational thought and an objective analytical perspective) and its primary psychological tool, insight. It can bring a certain amount of healing, self-understanding, and wisdom to our lives. But if we rely solely on the solar eye, then introspection may become a purely

---

2   William Blake, "The Marriage of Heaven and Hell," in *The Portable Blake*, ed. A. Kazin (New York: Penguin, 1976), 250.

rational endeavor and finally serve the ends of "I-want," thereby increasing the dominance of our egocentricity. Conceivably, it may be oriented both to the present and the future, solving problems in our psyche as we pursue what we want and what we think we need. It may be useful, leading to some soul-searching and even healing. But it remains a one-eyed perspective.

We may consider that Odin's trade for wisdom was not a straight-out barter, but a sacrifice, a reorientation leading to a more balanced form of vision. Odin became the god of fate by dedicating one eye to the hag and her source of water, the spirit of life, deep within the dark of the earth. Indeed, wisdom requires an eye looking out and an eye looking in, one looking forward and one looking back. Seeing through the growth cycles and the life cycle to their true depths may require the old woman and the deep spring—or, in terms of the classic metaphor—the active sun and the passive earth.

Reflection takes us inward and back, across the interior landscape of our life's journey and even through the heritage of our ancestors. We return to our beginnings and earlier experiences with the consciousness of today. We return until we have taken psychological responsibility for our previous unconscious actions—actions that were then outside the realm of our intentional control and whose meanings were therefore lost to us.

Reflection allows the pieces to fall into place in the chronicle of our life and in the nature of life, balancing our insight. We return until we weave the experiences of our life and our fate and their emotional consequences into the patterns of our destiny and begin to comprehend what life wants of us. This activity sounds religious, sacred, but it is valued minimally and only by a few in our society, a society focused on extroversion, identity, and productivity. This is our societal mindset and it refuses to confront Odin's ancient choice.

Reflection and insight can combine, enriching introspection as a process for bringing us new understandings. What was formerly a block, an addiction, a psychological problem, or an illness may now be transformed into a personal moral problem. "Knowing what we are doing" sounds like taking action based on insight, careful analysis, and planning, and on the solar level, this perspective is true. But on a deeper level, through the vision of both eyes after the deepening choice has been made, "knowing what we are doing" means perceiving the truth of our own nature and consciousness and then living as congruently as possible with this knowledge. Insight balanced with reflection brings us onto the razor's edge of living.

Many people seek Jungian analysis because they long for wholeness and relief from life's tensions. They want their difficulties to be valued, to be thought of as more than deficiencies within themselves or as psychic infections. They wish to transform their tensions and difficulties into a vision that will lead to richer meaning in their lives. Too often, however, they expect the analyst to have a simple formula that will lead to *easy* meaning. Simplicity and easiness go out the window when we begin to realize that the faults we have been projecting onto others are faults embedded within ourselves. Most people continue through this tough experience of realization and then find, within themselves and life, the enrichment that was previously blocked. In fact, quite a few people come into analysis for this very reason.

In many instances, we must take the anger, resentment, hurt, jealousy, or even love and adoration—the energy we have projected outward—and hold it within ourselves. Such a holding is required to be in a container that is conscious, insightful, and reflective in order to prevent it from becoming self-destructive. In other words, holding it must not be confused with repressing it, which would be to hold it unconsciously and defensively. Our emotional heat, generated by the tension, the suffering from holding these things unconsciously, will provide the impetus for the inner alchemy of transformation and assimilation to begin.

Not only must we overcome the shock of self-discovery and have the strength to accept it but we must also wrestle with ourselves as Jacob wrestled with the dark angel—until a new day dawns, a new psychological standpoint is reached, a river is crossed—and we reconcile with a disassociated part of ourselves. Our faults and sins, usually small in our own perception, once acknowledged fully, may soon appear to be the advance guard of barbaric hordes threatening our psychic kingdom. They may frighten us back into the safety of our conventional citadels, leaving us childishly afraid of venturing into life.

True self-knowledge always requires a moral choice to accept or reject greater consciousness. To authentically face such a choice in the context of the society in which we live and have developed, we must return to our interior and develop our *feeling function*.[3] Without a well-developed feeling function, we cannot discriminate between what is important in our life and what is not. If we do not have a personal value system anchored deep within ourselves, our life cannot reflect our authenticity. In the absence of this value system, we cannot even choose what consciousness to keep and what to discard. Without a mature feeling function, we cannot take a stand for what is personal and what is of value. If we lack the ability to take such a stance, reflection and eros will always be overrun by the perceived demands and practicalities in our lives. Accepting new consciousness requires devotion, courage of the heart in the spirit of life, the willingness to accept suffering and despair, and our enduring the cycle of transformation.

Rilke remarked, "One lives badly because one always comes in to the present unfinished, unable, distracted." He is expressing a universal sentiment in these lines, one that sneaks up on each of us. At some time or another, we wish we had undergone a better or more complete formation. We wish our parents had done a better job, that our teachers had been wiser and more sensitive. We wish we had been more aware of the choices we were making.

While I understand the sentiment that Rilke expresses as a common experience, I don't accept its truth. I believe it can be

---

3 This is the Jungian term for the psychological function used to make decisions based on a personal value system. It will be further explained in later pages.

dangerous, because this longing can lead us to evaluate life on the wrong level. Our bona fide transformation, as well as our destiny, resides within our ability to muster the wherewithal for a lifelong process of psychological re-forming. In fact, re-forming our story in the light of present consciousness is simply our voluntary participation in the process of life as it moves through us. Each re-formation alters our horizon and extends the boundaries of our personality in a manner that is never lost again. To be finished, able, and undistracted would mean to be perfect, and being perfect in any form leaves us without a future—with no more potential for transformation, no more chances for being human.

As I have mentioned, there is a final step. Self-knowledge, understanding, and even re-formation mean little when viewed from afar. They must be grasped and lived, lived fully and vitally as part of our life-process. Success in the art of living is the result of having been in psychological danger, having gone through the experience to the end, and then having reflected on it. Full participation must precede understanding, for only the life that has been lived can be known. Such participation requires so much devotion that little room is left for the distance that is a part of detached observation and comparisons. This approach does not mean living foolishly. It leaves plenty of room for judgment, thinking, and feeling evaluations. And the farther we go in this journey, the more personal it becomes. We find ourselves becoming artists, and what we create is our own lives.

To say we must learn from experience sounds so simple. Even our parents told us that. Indeed, we learn surface lessons from the pain or happiness resulting from our actions. But if that's all we learn, we have failed to recognize that a life that "works" isn't necessarily fulfilling. For life to be fulfilling, we must learn from experience by reflecting upon experience, looking for the deeper implications of the patterns and their meanings in our life.

Our reflection is based on the desire to live, to participate fully and faithfully in the experience of our own life. From the interior standpoint, if we are thoughtful, our greatest psychological fear is that we will fail to live our personal pattern of life. We desire a life that journeys toward its inherent completion and we fear an incomplete life. For this reason, death can become a friend that substantiates our life. It travels beside us, urging our reflection. It stands before us representing the hope of completion and it stands behind us representing our fear of a life that passed but was not lived. Eros and Thanatos, life and death, mill us between them as our hidden teacher tries to force our life to be a journey of growth and discovery rather than a well-mapped conventional trip around the block.

Chapter 2

THE QUEST FOR LIFE

Birth

During our birth, we moved from darkness into light. We were expelled from a dark, warm, pulsating, nurturing, saline environment into the harsh light of outer life. The Greeks referred to birth as *krysis*, meaning a separation. Indeed, we come to the dawn of our lives in crisis, compelled to separate from safety by the very nature that so warmly conceived and nurtured us. Many depth psychologists (those who deal with the unconscious) as well as other theorists refer to this experience symbolically as our being expelled from the Garden of Eden.

According to Otto Rank, an early colleague of Freud[1] (who went on to develop his own theories), our birth is the first heroic journey we make. In many ways it is also the simplest, since we have little choice in the matter—we must traverse the *krysis* whether we want to or not.

Esther Harding,[2] one of the first Jungian[3] analysts and theorists, describes two kinds of traditional heroes—the divine or semi-

---

1 Sigmund Freud was the founder of psychoanalysis, promoting a therapy based on dialogue between the analyst and patient. Among others, he introduced the concepts of the ego and id.

2 M. Esther Harding, the first U.S. Jungian psychoanalyst, was a prolific author and educator.

3 Carl Gustav Jung developed the school of analytical psychology. His concepts include introversion, extraversion, and the collective unconscious.

divine hero and the entirely human hero, weak and fallible, not even aware he is setting out on a heroic task. We enter life that second way, like Jonah being spit out on the beach. If we are lucky, we enter into a family environment that momentarily recreates our former blissful experience. This gives us the chance to develop a certain amount of trust in the world we have been thrust into and, more or less, a chance to learn to feel at home in it. We don't have to be born into a perfect family in order to develop this trust—we need only a certain threshold of love and security. On the other hand, we may be cast, paradoxically, by the hand of *grace* into a cauldron that will be the foundation of our destiny—if we can ever get a grip on it.

Such a paradox—being born into a traumatic situation rather than a peaceful one—is hard to appreciate in terms of its face value. But if we can recall our mythological heritage, we may begin to understand that the stories of life support this very point. The mythological hero is usually born into a divided family or into a family that is under some extreme threat. For example, Moses was put into the bulrushes for safety; King Arthur was placed with a stepfamily so he would not be murdered as a child; Parsifal, who found the Holy Grail, had a missing father; Zeus, who brought order to the Greek cosmos, had a devouring father.

The point is that being born into a horrible or undesirable situation can either cripple us emotionally, destroy us; or the circumstances, if they are in some way right, can call forth the creative strength of the human spirit and forge a remarkable person. In such a case, we are embroiled from the beginning in those circumstances that will be the focus of our life's personal pattern.

In contrast to that kind of intensity, most births set us on the general path of predictable developmental events. As we evolve a beginning sense of identity and commence our cognitive growth, we create the illusion that we are in control of, or are taking control of, our life. As this development transpires, we lose touch with our instinctual embeddedness in life's patterns and the lines of nature that guide, regulate, and direct our maturation. In forming our illusion of control, we most likely haven't developed any sense of our personal pattern and probably won't for a long time. Our awareness of the patterns of our existence lies far back in the mists of our undeveloped psyche. (We must also remember that neither the fates nor our life's patterns mean we are predestined to this or that, or are simply victims of life. We do make choices, and so do others, and our choices affect us and, in some manner, all those around us.)

The fact is, our modern minds are not as bright as we like to think they are, as we have lost our vision of life and how it grows.

The Search for Identity

Once we are born, the symbolic dawn of childhood begins. Childhood is the bedrock of our personality, the foundation of how we relate to ourselves and the world. As children, we develop in two ways simultaneously. We develop physical skills and we also develop a sense of identity, of psychological *form*.

This quest for identity is both personal and collective. Thus, as history evolves, human beings in general seek an always-becoming collective identity along the lines of life's general pattern. This quest is also carried forward by each of us as individuals, in every generation, in terms of our personal path.

Jung used the term "psyche" (meaning the whole of our being, conscious and unconscious, body and spirit) in contrast to the more commonly used term, "personality" (which usually refers to personal characteristics or traits in a manner that ignores spirit and often ignores important components of our unconscious mind as well as our body). The breadth of this definition of psyche is important if we want to understand our own childhood, because childhood occurrences are not simply cognitive events. The dramatic circumstances of childhood live on in our emotions, our temperament, and our body as well as in our mind—they are "structured" into our personality by our experiences. That is why we cannot simply leave them behind, think them away, and "get on with our lives." We must return again and again to locate our roots. Each time we do, we will find the energy to carry us more fully into the experience of living. Each time, we will become less dominated by the events that formed us.

This process is particularly important if we have been harshly wounded in childhood, if we have been rejected or otherwise traumatized by our parents. Such wounds shake, and may destroy, our trust in the world. If these wounds are deep enough, they may leave us detached from our own nature, cut off from the reality of our feelings and experiences. As a result, we may live either in an idealized fantasy world or in an emotional hell of depression and anxiety. Neither is real, even though we experience it as though it were.

When either of these things happens, our ability to relate to life realistically has been repressed into what Jung called the shadow side of our personality. Ordinarily, our shadow consists of the inferior (traits or qualities we are not good at and therefore we try to avoid developing), uncivilized (socially undesirable), and animal (baser instinctual) qualities of our personality. They are the qualities we repress in order to fit our identity into the conventional molds put forward by our family and culture. However, if our family and others in our environment disapprove of a particular quality or are brutal, threatening, or anxious and disturbed, we may also repress our *best* qualities in an effort to draw as little attention to ourselves as possible. As a result, we will have disassociated from our capacity for a normal life. At this point, our life's work, psychologically, becomes a crusade for our own existence and for the courage to mourn our cruel beginnings.

In some cases, childhood wounds may be deep enough to destroy a person. But in less extreme cases, difficult childhoods often contribute to the redemption of culture by giving us extrasensitive, creative people. If we examine the lives of outstanding individuals in almost any field—politics, art, business, and so on—the greatest ones almost always come from homes that were in some way troubled. Whether Beethoven or Churchill, Roosevelt or MacArthur, DaVinci or Emily Dickinson, we find the mythological pattern of a challenging development calling forth the spirit of their particular talents to create their destiny. Further, because all of us are wounded to some extent, mourning needs to be reincorporated as an accepted, necessary, and respected part of our culture, for we all suffer as a result of living. In fact, Joseph Campbell, the well-known authority on mythology, observes that the quester is precisely a person who *has* failed, because his or her life does not work. Interior difficulties force questers to reorganize their life on a higher level, to become, out of necessity, adept at the art of living.

The idea that the way to peace is through adversity runs contrary to the way many of us were brought up. However, harmony and the absence of conflict are not necessary conditions for peace. In fact, if we blindly cling to the notion that they are, we will create a psychological world that *must* explode in our faces, and this explosion is often acted out in the lives of our children. Such an illusory vision of peace leaves us unable to appreciate the world we actually live in and to celebrate life. We have to accept life's imperfections and be at home in them. Otherwise, we deny the cycles of existence, lose our opportunities for meaning, love, and truth, and live as ghosts, both longing for and fearing some future substantiation of our vitality and spiritual potential rather than living now. Pursuing harmony, like pursuing happiness on a shallow level, often robs us of our potential for joy and fulfillment.

The true way to peace is to recognize that our childhood, whether we were happy or not, whether we *think* we were happy or not, was not truly a peaceful time. Our boundaries were fragile. We depended entirely on others for our physical, emotional, and spiritual well-being, and these others often hurt us, either maliciously or unintentionally. And yet childhood, no matter how bad it may have been, is not a disease to be cured. Because it is the foundation of our life and the beginning of our soul's incarnation, we cannot entirely dissolve or correct its pain by psychological treatment. We can only digest that pain and incorporate it.

Our real struggle is to find a conscious relationship to our own childhood, no matter what it was like. This struggle may call for healing and understanding, but neither of these attainments will count if we cannot also come into a conscious relationship with that period in our life. We must be separate from our childhood—not dominated by its emotional tenor and its events—but we must be connected to it as well. Like it or not, we should see it as the cornerstone of our life, hoping eventually to transform it into a friend, if it is not one already. In Chapter 8, in the section titled "Shalom," you will find a very good example of this process, given by a man reflecting on his analytic work.

The Second Birth—Becoming "I"

As we grow into adolescence we continue to build our sense of identity, shaped now not only by our family and friends but also by school, religious institutions, and the media. And in order to build our identity, we have to differentiate between what is "I" and what is "not-I" (in Esther Harding's terms). As "I" takes control in our personality, we have to repress and disassociate from our threatening, primitive inner nature and its extreme emotions, which can drive us into regrettable behaviors. Like Zeus subduing the Titans and giants, we battle to become the master in our own little cosmos.

This process, again, is not a peaceful one. By now, we should clearly understand that to be human is to have conflict, although few of us learn this fact despite the fact that we continually live it. Some objective knowledge and wisdom can be passed on from person to person, but each of us must travel through the pain and conflict to create the form we need to hold it. If we don't do this at the beginning of our journey and become strengthened travelers, we will spend the second half of our journey through life wandering in the psychological wastelands. This is not necessarily bad, since many people find their way out of the wastelands and are better for the experience. But it is dangerous, because some do become hopelessly lost. Their lives slip out from under them and they don't even know it. They may even be glad to see their lives end.

In order to come into form, we have to follow a basic law of living among others that was discovered early on by Adam—to eat, we must work. In modern times, this means we have to construct a personality and a public face (persona) that is acceptable and workable in society. The problem is, we have to do this while, at the same time, we are trying to construct a sense of individual identity. As the word "form" implies, coming into our personality requires a certain amount of conformity, which means putting aside self-centered attitudes—not an easy task, as adolescence is a very self-centered time of life. All sorts of instincts are boiling over at this time, and adolescents are full of impulsiveness, creativity, and even spirituality, as well as the need for personal freedom.

Since young adults see their qualities of nonconformity, idealism, and detachment from parental values as the very essence of their personal identity, many teenagers feel they must annihilate themselves in order to fit the *conventional form* "authority" dictates, which is the great crisis of adolescence. The songs, stories, and poems of teenagers reflect how they feel about this crisis. Today's teenagers show a fascination with rebellion, suicide, murder, and death. Some of this response is natural, but most of it reflects our failure as parents, and especially fathers, to initiate our young into life in a healthier way—a way that strengthens them and gives them the courage and desire to win life, as the mythological heroes had to win the bride from the dragon.

Sharon, for example, was an adolescent girl with whom I had been working for several months. She was the daughter of divorced parents and unable to articulate the deep despair she felt. For many years her parents had shipped her back and forth between their homes at their convenience as they tried out new lovers and new marriages.

Sharon walked quietly into her afternoon session, offering no greetings, only silence. As usual, she was staring at the floor. She meekly sat down without lifting her eyes. Then suddenly, for the first time in our work, she looked straight into my face. Tears streamed down her cheeks. She thrust the following poem into my hand and said, "This is how I feel." Slowly, I read it.

About School[4]

He always wanted to say things. But no one understood.
He always wanted to explain things. But no one cared.
So he drew...
And it was all of him. And he loved it.
When he started school he brought it with him. Not to show
*   anyone, but just to have it with him like a friend.*
It was funny about school.
He sat in a square, brown desk like all the other square, brown
*   desks, and he thought it should be red.*
And his room was a square, brown room. Like all the other rooms.
*   And it was tight and close. And stiff...*

The teacher came and spoke to him. She told him to wear a tie
*   like all the other boys. He said he didn't like them and she*
*   said it didn't matter.*
After that they drew. And he drew all yellow and it was the
*   way he felt about the morning. And it was beautiful.*
The teacher came and smiled at him. "What's this?" she said.
*   "Why don't you draw something like Ken's drawing?*
Isn't that beautiful?"
It was all questions.
And he threw the old picture away.
And when he lay out alone looking at the sky, it was big and
*   blue and all of everything, but he wasn't anymore.*
He was square inside and brown, and his hands were stiff, and
*   he was like anyone else. And the thing inside him that*
*   needed saying didn't need saying anymore.*
It had stopped pushing. It was crushed. Stiff.
Like everything else.

---

4   This poem, which I have abbreviated, was circulating at her school. I have
     no knowledge of the author. The rumor that went around with the poem
     was that it was by a 17-year-old boy who killed himself shortly after having
     written it.

When I finished reading it, I quietly looked back into her eyes. "I know," I said. "I know."

Our first encounter with the unseen social power demanding to shape our lives, the one captured in this poem, is the opening skirmish of a struggle that is lifelong for all of us. If we are to live vitally and creatively, we will always be torn between the individual and the others. We must try to hold our center in the conflict without falling into unthinking conformity on the one hand or existential despair on the other—which is why adolescence should be a quest for life as well as for form. That is what desire and eros are all about.

Sexuality is the raw instinctual power of the species. It reflects nature's purpose on a level so powerful and basic that we often fear it almost as much as death. And sexuality explodes into the lives of youth today in a more terrifying manner than ever before. What was once contained in sacred vessels, guided by traditions taught to the young from the wisdom of the elders, now threatens to smash their hard-won form, drive them beyond reason, and jeopardize their personal existence, literally and figuratively.

But eros can also instruct. It brings us to the basic question: how can I be a man, how can I be a woman, what if I feel I'm not quite meant to be either? Beyond that, we can discover the meaning of the powerful urge that drives us, against all odds, toward a single vision of life, no matter how distant and inaccessible it may be. Properly faced and channeled, this urge can result in great creativity and a renewed sense of vitality and aesthetics that can make a major contribution to personal and cultural experience. Additionally, it can give our life an incomparable unity, leading us to pursue a goal that enriches us even if we never attain it, or if we attain it and lose it again. Too bad the wise old ones are no longer here to help us see through this drama. (And, practical as they are, sex education classes, self-help books, and the offices of sex therapists rarely offer the deeper answers, the life answers.)

The social aspects of eros, of the fundamental vitality and force of life, propel us toward identity and move us on toward the goals of sexuality and human relationships. The psychological component of eros leads us toward the goal of inner unification through a union of the masculine and feminine elements in our personality.[5] In Jungian psychology, these relationships also symbolize the union of the conscious personality with the unconscious, which brings a feeling of wholeness to our psyche. These dynamics of eros are born in the conflicts of adolescence, but they remain the basic material of a life's work.

This may be why sexuality and relationships are still the primary issues that bring most people in for psychotherapy or analysis. Like adolescents, many patients I've seen attempt to control their sexual instincts by becoming spiritually obsessed or they avoid their spirituality by becoming sexually or materially obsessed. They may also either denigrate or idolize relationships. Often, one or both people involved in such relationships have withdrawn from the field of life and relationship by sublimating their vitality into another direction, such as a career, an addiction, depression, or some other overly self-absorbed dimension. More often than not, I can get a fairly accurate psychological picture of people just from discovering the kinds of emotional attachments they are involved in.

Purpose

Becoming separate and differentiated is the first step in the long journey through adolescence. The equally important next step is to develop self-confidence and a place in the world.

The initiation rites of ancient cultures developed a sense of unity and direction in initiates through a shared sense of instruction,

---

5   It is pretty well known today that Jung considered that each personality contains an inner image of the opposite sex—the anima (or inner feminine image) in the man's personality and the animus (or inner masculine image) in the woman's personality. These images appear in dreams and fantasies and are projected onto individuals of the opposite sex, most often when we fall in love. This element in our personality is an inner guide and offers many creative possibilities in our development. Therefore, our interior relationship to it is very important.

suffering, and sacrifice. Young people today, however, have grown up far from these roots—they feel separate and alone in their struggle for identity, when they need to feel separate and together. Adolescence is the time when they need to discover a cause greater than themselves, a purpose that will bring a deep and satisfying sense of oneness, a purpose beyond simple personal ambitions and material concerns.

We used to call such purposes "goals," but our cursory, literal definitions of goals and how to "achieve them" in every sphere—personal, business, societal, and even religious—has robbed the word "goal" of its more profound meaning, its sense of true purpose. But that other, original kind of goal—a true purpose—will help us become oriented in the world, filling our lives with meaning as well as with the confidence in the future.

Alfred Adler, another colleague of Freud (who also developed his own theory), noted that we cannot think, feel, or act without a purpose. As we grow from one state of life to another, that purpose is what allows us to evaluate our progress toward increased awareness, higher consciousness, and more balanced living. It leads us into fresh, vigorous starts and new meaning. If we do not live with such purpose, we either become lost and disoriented, or driven, as automatons, soldiering through life.

Soldiering through life as an automaton means refusing to live consciously and to take responsibility for ourselves. But we are made for conscious life and, if we refuse it, our inner voice will continue trying to get our attention, often aiming at our denial of life through dreams as well as through emotional and physical symptoms.

I recently worked with a middle-aged woman who dreamed that a rigid friend of hers had been poisoned by a witch. The witch was coming to poison her as well. As the poison was taking effect, the woman woke up screaming, "I don't want to die." Another analysand dreamed that, in order to avoid dying that night, all of the people on his street were to pin a note on their doors stating what the meaning of life was for them. He, himself, forgot to do this and realized his oversight too late. He rushed out the door and pleaded with God for another chance. God answered, "One more."

I believe we must listen to such dreams very carefully and avoid the temptation to over-analyze them. By accepting them with both feelings and attention, understanding them through the heart as well as the mind, we have a better chance of discovering how to bring the message into our life. And, bringing such a message into life is the important work we must do.

If we are living lives that are without purpose and dreams don't reach us, a depression, an illness, or an acting-out adolescent may be required if we are to lower our resistance enough to hear our inner voice. But even then, we can choose to turn a deaf ear to ourselves.

Many analysts have worked with people who sought them out during a crisis or because of frightening dreams and then abruptly stopped coming. Often these people stop as soon as the emotional pressure eases up a little. They seem to intuit that new unconscious material is about to erupt, requiring the emergence of a new consciousness on their part, and they quickly look for a rationale for escaping the confrontation. They want to remain the same selves they've always been, doing the same things they have been doing, except that they want to be *happy*. They usually explain their departure by saying something like, "I really appreciate you and enjoyed working with you, but analysis is just too expensive." They have missed the chance to find purpose in their lives during this experience.

Youth, however, hunger for this experience of purpose. They badger us incessantly about social and political issues. (Religious issues are now too distant, except in a few cases.) They not only want purpose for themselves, but they want it for us also. They want to engage us, break our molds, and have us return to a point at which we are living for more than our daily bread. They hunger for parents who have gone before them in the world, parents who are not afraid of the great questions of life. They want us to teach them spiritual initiatives and creativity in the art of living. If we don't or can't, they'll slip into their own renegade culture and find a sense of spiritual oneness by rebelling against our values. Their spiritual and psychological initiation will follow, in the cults of gangs, drugs, sex, and other peer movements.

Practical parents are mystified by this self-destructive behavior because practical parents miss the point. Yes, they advise their children how to find a good job, a good house, a good family, good social standing. But such direction ignores the importance of the moral problems on which our well-being as human beings depends. If we are to mature, we need to establish a sense of purpose in the world. Living with purpose produces competence in us, and as our journey continues, purpose will also give us the strength we require to search for the values of the human soul. We must search for a higher level of consciousness than the one at which our generation is now living, a level to which nature and civilization demand that we aspire.

Remembering Ourselves

Symbolically, the child and the youth we once were live on within us, and at each major transition point in life we may need to return to their perspective. This doesn't mean we should idolize them though, for these tumultuous stages of life were far from ideal. Instead, we should let our images of these stages represent new life, regardless of our present age. In times of inner change, some of which we are not consciously aware of yet, the youth returns in our dreams. We may dream of a schoolchild, reminding us of inner preparation; or, as despair is turning into creation, we may dream of infants, new life, or being born.

We must create a *form* for the life in us, a form in which our life can grow, mature, expand, create, and feel secure. We give this form different names—personality, identity, ego, and persona—according to our perspective. But we must remember that the form never lasts. Sooner or later, life evolves or rebels, and we must start again as our personality continues to grow. Hopefully, we are rooted powerfully enough in our own ground and have a strong enough relationship to our beginnings to withstand the inner tempest of this evolution.

The archetypal path of transformation, of building new forms as the old ones are outgrown, underlies the development of the human personality. This pattern is summarized as *birth, change, and death*, moving along in an eternal cycle. And this cycle is not only symbolically true in regard to psychological stages, but it is also concretely true in regard to all life. Life moves us along whether we like it or not, whether we consciously choose growth or not. Either way, if we open our eyes, we see that life and growth are not peaceful. There is plenty of conflict.

Many of us leave the essential conflicts of life's evolution to themselves. We simply assume the conflicts will pass and that the psychological conditions of childhood, the bedrock of our perceptions and values, will persist throughout our lives. We then end up stunned and amazed when they do not—although they never have. Still, most of us don't open our eyes early on. Anyway, it's not yet time. During late adolescence and young adulthood, we need to proceed as if we know where we are going.

Chapter 3

THE PASSAGE INTO ADULTHOOD

Identity—The Basic Fault

The history of our collective development reflects many characteristics of our personal development. In fact, Jung postulated that we all carry this collective history in our unconscious. We find that studying the history of humanity, particularly as it relates to our origins, is helpful to us in understanding some of these personal processes. We can also see how intricately connected our inner and outer lives are, as well as our personal and collective ones. All four of these aspects of life seem to be interdependent in their progression, shaping and forming each other. A look at history may help illustrate a crucial point that we experience in our development into young adulthood.

As Western history progressed, the Roman goddess of peace, Pax, proved to be just as nebulous as her Greek predecessor, Eirene. Pax Romana meant no more than the absence of strife and the sensation of quiet, both at home and abroad. To achieve it the Romans imposed order on the world as they knew it, and this order allowed the gods to be in their temples, the farmers in their fields, the merchants in their shops, and the philosophers in their towns. But, as Seneca remarked, whole tribes and peoples were uprooted, displaced, repressed, and sacrificed to the establishment of Pax Romana.

Peace had a similar meaning in the Old Testament world. Peace in this Near Eastern area was a social concept that meant well-being and prosperity for the family, the city, and the nation. As with the Romans, the Hebrews justified war in the pursuit of peace. In both cases, peace depended on the separation of the world into *us* and *them*, whether *they* were Philistines or barbarians. The God who commanded, "Thou shalt not kill" did not seem concerned about killing *them* and even directed such wars. This polarization shows how deep and paradoxical the division of Western human nature against itself has been. Even today, people who are uncultured, boorish, and indifferent to *our* artistic and cultural values are called barbarians or philistines.

Paradoxically, the cultures that imposed peace on the "others" nevertheless found some of the truest values of humanity in the people they conquered. In the *Iliad*, Hector is the leading spiritual hero, and the Trojan story contains many poignant moments, gentle and human. During this grand conflict, even the gods were split in their various loyalties. In Roman history, many similar moments occurred. The Romans' admiration for Hannibal was enormous, which didn't prevent the destruction of his city. In Hebrew literature, Ruth the Canaanite is the symbol of fidelity. The story of David and Bathsheba and of the murder of her husband shows that these issues are present as inner strife as well as outer.

We need to realize that as we enter into young adulthood, our interior Pax Romana, if we achieve it at all, does not come easily, and that when we *impose* it, we frequently subjugate some of our best and most authentic characteristics. In other words, to consolidate a personality that is independent and effective in society we must separate, conquer, sacrifice, repress, and suppress many parts of ourselves. While requiring the development of strength and focus, this process also bases our form, cohesiveness, and prosperity on our being ruthless to ourselves. We divide ourselves and push our "others" into fringe areas of our unconscious where, for a while, they are subjugated, denied, and alienated until they begin to turn toxic and, under certain circumstances, create discord. As history informs us, in terms of our general pattern, these areas usually turn out to be the source of future change and transformation.

For the rest of this chapter, I will examine this period of identity development in our lives and look at the meaning of its being both on-track and off. Understanding the process of becoming psychologically adjusted to the world and recognizing what parts of ourselves are included and excluded is necessary in order to gain access to an awareness of personal authenticity.

The Journey Continues

In our personal lives, the *krysis* of birth begins our painful journey into form. This journey carries us through childhood, where the journey takes on the nature of a search for identity. In this quest, our young ego has to battle the Titans and giants of the unconscious for control of our personality. We do this early in life, at age four or five, and the battle is reflected in our nightmares and fears of monsters under the bed and in the closets. We face a similar struggle again in adolescence, when so many of our emotions seem like giants and Titans—and the most fearful Titan of all is our extreme sensitivity to social acceptance and censure. In its own way, this struggle will show its face on every subsequent level of development we go through.

After our earliest challenges come the more visible crises of adolescence: the clashes between social norms and individual identity, social norms and eros, spiritually and eros, and the search for a purpose in all of these conflicts. If adolescence goes reasonably well, the next era of life—young adulthood—seems like a Pax Romana of the personality. Life is stable and orderly and we become effective in the world. We have a solid sense of identity.

But in spite of its apparent stability, this time still cannot be considered peaceful. It is filled with its own conflict, as was the Roman Empire. It requires that we strive toward some sort of success and keep a careful watch on warring, rebellious elements in the psyche. We must specialize—selecting certain attitudes and traits and a specific area of life on which to focus our energy. Certain attributes and attitudes become the "rulers and organizers" of our personality.

In order to specialize, we must ruthlessly split off and repress competing attitudes, desires, and talents. In order to be productive at one thing, we must put aside others. There are exceptions to this generality as a few of us seem to follow a compressed version of the journey and pass quickly into its later stages—maturity and wisdom following brilliant success at an early age. Albert Einstein's life was an example of such a journey. But this situation is rare, and most people who think they are moving at an accelerated pace have simply lost their ground and are spiraling upward into the realm of fantasy and self-delusion.

We must keep our personality one-sided at this stage in order to come to grips with life effectively. We simply cannot do everything at once. In the process, while we are developing ego strength and a robust persona (the "rulers"), we are also continuing to create our own shadow (the "others"). This area of our psyche contains the darker aspects of ourselves that did not fit the form and identity we chose to develop. The shadow is the place to which our Titans and giants have been banished, along with much of our barbarian and animal nature. And, depending on our circumstances, our noble Hector, our alluring Helen, our imposing Caesar, our pious Pope, or perhaps our religious fanatic as well as our criminal may also be found there, along with many others. Thus, our shadow contains characteristics that are both positive and negative. What must be clear by now is that for us to have an identity, to have substance in our personality and in the world, means inevitably that we also have a shadow.

The figures in our shadow are often paradoxical. Our self-righteous Pope, for example, may actually be our repressed longing for spirituality. And so, when we reach an emotional plateau after having compromised our lives too long, we may find in this shadow-land the disowned vitality we need for renewal. The energy of our unconscious criminal may reflect an outward life lived too rigidly in social conformity. But I am getting ahead of myself; this discussion will come later. The potential value or danger in our shadow figures is yet to be discovered in our life story.

Note, though, that ordinarily when we are in young adulthood, we are moving briskly, full of energy and anticipation. The era of public persona building is not as shallow as it sometimes may sound, and the identity we build, though one-sided, forms the foundation for future transformations. Anyone familiar with the collected letters of Dr. Jung knows how much his profession and family meant to him. They were his anchor in practical reality, giving him emotional security throughout the vigorous and often perilous inner journey that was his life. In her discussion of mysticism in the Western tradition, Evelyn Underhill, an Anglican scholar, points out that strength and form in the everyday world are the necessary ingredients for spiritual transformation. She writes, "It is not by the education of the lamb, but by the hunting and taming of the wild intractable lion, instinct with vitality, full of ardor and courage, exhibiting heroic qualities on the sensual plane, that the Great Work is achieved."[1]

A View of Life

To build this stable identity, we must do something. Usually that means that as we emerge from adolescence we try as best we can to decide where we're going with our lives. What we decide depends mostly on what society thinks is a meaningful life—in other words, on conventions. Such conventions often provide the best information we have. If we don't do anything—if we fail to make a choice—we run the risk of becoming eternal adolescents, always becoming but never being. On the other hand, though, we can become just as trapped in the role we have chosen. Usually that happens when we choose a role to compensate for some early wounding or when someone else really selects the role for us because of our lack of self-knowledge.

These risks aside, a conventional choice is not necessarily a bad one, and even a seemingly misdirected choice is not particularly tragic and may ultimately not really be important. We live in changing and confusing times and it's almost impossible to figure out one's lifetime goals at age twenty-one. The profession

1   Evelyn Underhill, *Mysticism: A Study in the Nature and Development of Man's Spiritual Consciousness* (New York: Meridian Books, 1974), 147.

I practice today was not available when I was that age. Besides, as Jung frequently said, if we do the wrong thing with energy and determination, we will eventually get to the right place as long as we try to maintain self-awareness and an openness to change.

The point is that we must find a place in the world in order for our journey to continue. If we have chosen the right thing to do, something we will stick with all of our lives, our relationship to it will change and evolve as our life proceeds. If we have chosen the wrong thing—if, as Joseph Campbell put it, we find we have climbed to the top of a ladder that is against the wrong wall—then we can always make other choices. In either case, making a choice is the first step toward a meaningful life. It is not the content of this choice that matters so much as the degree to which that choice establishes a foundation for the transformations that will make up our lives from that point on.

The choices we make are often shaped by eros, when it attracts us to others early in life. Family, children, and various social and business relationships follow, and these relationships involve us in responsibilities. Many things can interfere with our optimum development, however. In haste or fear we may consciously or unconsciously adopt a superficial ethic of opportunity, effectiveness, or getting on with it as our way of relating to life. This simplistic attitude will then color all of our relationships to others, ourselves, the world, and life. Or, in order to meet our responsibilities, we may have to dampen our soul's passion. The young scientist may have to set aside his passionate curiosity in order to publish more and get tenure. The young lawyer may have to defer a love of poetry to work on a brief that could lead to partnership.

Yet a passion of the soul must simmer below the level of our control if our life is ever going to become vital. In spite of our need to find a place in the world, eros must still be the connection to our ongoing experience. And desire, even when it is expressed as ambition, must be the prime mover. When eros and desire are denied, their shadow sides, fear and anxiety, either infect us with a dehumanizing drive or immobilize us. Paradoxically, however, the quest for a place in the world, which may lead us to set passions aside, can end up helping to create a vessel into which we can pour eros as life proceeds.

Retracing—Finding Our Lost Future

What if we are wounded in our childhood, along the lines of our discussion in Chapter 1? Practically speaking, because life is truly difficult, most of us *are* wounded to some extent or another during childhood. This wounding means we will have to return to that era and complete some healing work before our lives can express their true pattern.

People who have been emotionally wounded, often manage to find their way into conventional roles and relationships. They may achieve success in various fields, get married, and become parents. They can become active in community affairs and in the lives of their children and be thought of as good people. But behind closed doors, there may be serious problems with anger, anxiety, depression, sex, addictions, and other evidences of their inner distress.

Such people may follow the highways of collective endeavor very well, but at heart they are often still caught in childhood, usually trapped by their mother (I will discuss fathers later) in what psychologists call a mother complex. The archetypal image of the Mother/Wife is paradoxical. She calls us to life and to the service of life, but if we unconsciously personalize her, if her image dominates our sense of identity, we may take on the role of "my son, the doctor," or "my daughter, the lawyer," really meaning, "my son or daughter who lives his or her life only for others or other's expectations." Stability, responsibility, and prosperity are hallmarks of such people in the community—children a mother can be proud to claim—but they are likely to live as ghosts, cut off from their instinctual vitality and truth.

I once worked with a man who began to receive inner messages following a near-death experience in the ocean—he had almost drowned after being caught in a strong undertow. He was a professional who had been working in analysis in an effort to quit being an ideal son his mother could be proud of and to learn to be himself and then be proud of that. (To be ourselves, we must learn to rely on our instinctual responses to things rather than on social conventions to determine if they are truly valuable to us.) Being psychologically minded, he noticed that he had instinctively "struggled like mad" to live, far beyond the point of exhaustion. All the while, an impersonal voice in his head was saying, "You are going to die." A few days after his near-death experience, he decided to do a dialogue with the sea in his imagination, to develop a deeper understanding of himself. At one point in the dialogue, the sea said to him:

> Rely on your instincts and struggle like hell! Do something, even if it's wrong. Get in the current. Be willing to make a mess and be willing to live through it. Fight me and understand me. I am life.

At a later point in the dialogue, a crab appeared and told him it represented his desire for wealth, power, and sex, and that he had to live with and honor those desires. The steps on his personal journey required that he act as a full human being with human ambitions and desires, not as someone simply pursuing some ideal state.

Fathers, too, can drive their children into what, though it may seem from the outside like a healthy engagement with life, is actually only compensation. Having an identity based on pleasing or rebelling against their father often seems typical of sons. But daughters, in particular, are subject to this sort of drive. Often, they become their father's ideal companion because his eros is not developed enough to deal with more mature women, or because he wanted a son, or because the son he had was not the one he wanted. Early in their lives, many daughters learn to please their fathers excessively and get their attention. In the process, they may learn to excel in school, sports, or other activities he is fond of in order to please fathers who don't know how to truly value womanhood.

I think of a particular woman who came to me some time ago. For many years she had dreamed of a bull—huge, beautiful, powerful, and enraged. (In mythology, the bull has always represented the threatening excess of masculine power and its ability to dominate all aspects of life, especially those of feeling and caring.) In her dreams, her task was to tame him and she could only do so by making love to him. As we worked together, we discovered she was an "eternal maiden," naïve and undeveloped as a father's daughter, still imprisoned by his needs, though he was long dead. Her marriages, as one might expect, had been hell because she sought out men she could relate to in the way she did to her father, hoping for an affirmation that never came. Because she learned to achieve to please him, she appeared confident and successful in spite of her disastrous emotional life. The fact is that she has never developed her own mature identity and a persona that expresses who she is and could become. Her true self is still waiting for the healing necessary to emerge.

People who have been abused as children have their own problems in trying to make a place for themselves in the world. They may be so caught up in addictions, rage, terror, and anti-social problems that they are incapable of functioning. Or they may enter into a marriage searching for compensation in an ideal "soul mate," or start a family they intend to make into the perfect family. Then, when they fail to find their ideal, they may become withdrawn, hiding their small flame of individuality and vitality deep within some inner cavern or in acting-out behavior.

Jungian psychology deals with wounds by, paradoxically, amplifying rather than reducing our problems. It declares that dreams and symptoms exist for a purpose. They are there to lead us back to the path we have lost, to meaning, to truth, and to the art of living. This is in contrast to conventional counseling and psychotherapy, which, even if humanistic, often work to make problems go away in the name of self-actualization, realizing one's full potential, or living triumphantly. This triumphant approach, though appealing, ignores one key lesson of centuries of psychospiritual wisdom. We are most authentically human when we are able honestly to see and honestly to love all that is faulted, lame, or damaged in ourselves. The woman I just described didn't need to kill or banish her bull. She needed to tame him with eros, for her own love was needed to heal her woundedness. Likewise, with all of us, our own love is needed to heal our woundedness. Wisdom comes from suffering and the human spirit is tempered in the fires of life. Balance is more likely to come by exploring our faults and by discovering the treasure in our shadow than by trying to deny them or overcome them with shallow techniques.

In support of this position, I would like to tell an ancient Italian fairy tale about a wolf (a story I have heard but could never find in written form). In former times, when forests were vast, according to the story, there lived a huge and ferocious wolf. This wolf seemed to delight in killing not only the chickens and the livestock of the village but also, from time to time, a villager. Old people and children were its customary prey, but it seemed to fear no one. The villagers tried in vain to poison, capture, or kill this wolf, but were unsuccessful. They called for hunters from near and far to hunt it. Elegant noblemen with great horses, packs of hounds, and many retainers tried to help them, but the wolf managed to evade them all.

Finally, the village elders, in desperation, sent a message to St. Francis, imploring his help in getting rid of this beast. St. Francis came immediately to their aid. He arrived at the village then set out for the wolf's lair without eating or resting. He journeyed deep into the forest, perhaps farther than anyone had gone before. There he found the wolf. They stood before each other, eye to eye, for some time, then St. Francis said simply, "Brother Wolf."

When St. Francis returned to the village, the villagers gathered around him in great excitement and begged him to tell them how to deal with the wolf.

He said to them, "Feed it."

For many of us, childhood wounds are our personal wolves. We cannot deny them or pray them away. We cannot grieve and heal them away, either. To lose them is to lose ourselves, for they are a part of our foundation. We must face them, make them brothers or sisters, and feed them. In other words, we must come into relationship with them, which may—incidentally—include healing, praying, and grieving.

Young adulthood, the midmorning of our lives, is a time of building. It is an outer-world time. Most of us do complete its tasks, later if not sooner. The peace of this time is a provisional peace, an outer peace that puts the things of the world in regulated perspective and in controlled relationships. Eros, emotions, spirituality, ambition, relationships, desire, individuality—all the components of human life—are in their proper homes, temples, schools, office parks, and shopping centers. At least for the time being.

Chapter 4

ENCOUNTERING LIFE

Discovering We Have Lost Our Compass

In today's world we have to *intend* to become adults. With affluence, birth control, and an absence of societal expectations, supportive rituals, and customs, our remaining in emotional childhood for extra decades and even for life has become easy. Nobody else can make this choice for us—this choice to become an adult—as adults in primitive tribes made it for their initiates. We no longer have outer circumstances that can save us from the necessity to make this choice personally. Driver's licenses, school graduations, sports teams, Boy Scout and Girl Scout activities, Outward Bound-type programs, menstrual cycles, and even pregnancies cannot bring about maturity on their own.

A successful arrival in adulthood means we have developed our personality into a cohesive form and we have taken up the mantle of a role, a place in the world that has a purpose. These activities reflect psychological maturity and bring about a change of attitude. Adulthood means we have become psychologically self-responsible, having left the state of non-responsibility and dependency that marks childhood and other youthful stages.

By the time we have achieved a purpose, a stable identity, and a place in the world, we may want to stop and breathe a sigh of relief. But life continues to push us with the imperative to grow and become. The fact is, we have found the common gold and are nearing completion of the tasks of the first half of our life and the beginning of the work of the second half.

This turning point comes to us unannounced, accompanied by small amounts of discomforting awareness. Generally, by our late thirties, we may begin discovering that the world we are living in is not quite the way we thought it was. The person we fell in love with turns out to be very different from what we had imagined and may actually seem like a stranger. The career that seemed so engaging turns out to be dull and almost pointless. As we make these discoveries, we may begin to wonder about the other aspects of our life. The kids who are keeping our house in turmoil seem like they must either be someone else's or creatures from another planet. And if we ask around, we may discover that our close friends, colleagues, and family members are beginning to wonder about us as well. Beneath the orderly surface of our lives, a current of emotional confusion is developing.

This confusion, however, is perfectly natural, for one of the great *boundary* situations of life is approaching and, psychologically, we are preparing for the crossing.

The first step in this preparation is a shift in our perceptions, a shift that usually begins before we're aware of it, which leaves us wondering who we are and what we are doing with our life. Often we experience the shift as a feeling of being trapped and living a warmed-over existence, as if we had missed the chance to live out our true selves. A lot of people, naturally, are terrified of the approach of the midday of life.

Boundaries

We began life through the *krysis* of birth, our first great boundary crossing. As the journey continued, we came to many other important crossings. The ancients recognized these boundaries; called them Childhood, Youth, Adulthood, and Old Age; and marked each with rituals and initiation ceremonies. As modern life has increased in complexity, we have added many smaller crossings, such as graduating from grammar school, middle school, high school, and college; changing jobs; divorce; and so on. Each of these crossings still requires that, to a greater or lesser extent, we participate in the heroic cycle of the decline and death of old attitudes and the birth of new ones.

This heroic cycle, as chronicled by Joseph Campbell, begins with a call. We experience such a call either when we are facing one of the great boundary situations of life or when our life, for whatever reason, is simply not working. As the call begins, we may feel frustrated, restless, anxious, and depressed. Then as it continues to pull at us, we may feel fragmented and confused, as activities that used to challenge us lose their flavor.

Campbell was fond of using the Grail legend to illustrate this point. In this legend, King Arthur had spent many years organizing his Knights of the Round Table, consolidating his country, and bringing peace and justice to the realm. Once these tasks were accomplished, little remained for the knights to do. As a result, they became restless, bored, and quarrelsome. Being a knight had lost its zing. This circumstance led to the discovery of the wasteland, representing, as you might guess, the wasteland within ourselves. The wasteland represents the parts of ourselves that were wounded, necessarily or unnecessarily, to support our adaptation and development. The result was the call to a new type of activity for the knights, the quest for the Holy Grail. This new quest, according to Campbell, represented the individual spiritual quest to renew the meaning, wholeness, and vitality of life.

In the old rituals, initiates undergoing a rite of passage left the place where they lived their daily lives and entered a ritual space. Then, when they had completed their transformation, they returned to normal life. Their new status was generally celebrated by their community. Today, the people around us barely notice when we are faced with a boundary crossing, and we must go through the processes more or less alone. Thus, once we become aware of what's going on in us, we must, usually without much assistance from others, create a sacred space inside ourselves. And when the process of transformation is over, we must return to the "house" of our personality. (This process may show up in dreams of living in a new house or even a new neighborhood.)

One of Campbell's major points in regard to the Grail quest is that it is now an individual matter. Each knight must enter the forest alone, meaning each of us must enter our own experience—the forest of our own emotions and our own unconscious—and find our own way. Analysts and psychotherapists can help if they have experienced their own quest in this manner. But such persons, as well as legends and mythological heroic motifs, can only acquaint us with general patterns of life. We must then discover our own personal life pattern within these contexts.

After the boundary crossing, we have a new attitude, a different level of consciousness, and perhaps different ideals and perspectives—but we aren't finished. The final step in the cycle requires us to integrate our new self with our old. We must maintain a relationship to our own history, for it is the landscape of our homeland. After each crossing, we must return to our history and rework our relationship to it based on who we have now become. Working out this relationship is the only way we can feel at home in ourselves.

Some years ago, I worked with a woman who, through many difficult years of analysis, managed to weather a stormy journey of change that lasted virtually her entire adult life. The daughter of a raging, sexually abusive, alcoholic father, she had married a man with a similar disposition, as many such daughters do. In a surge of midlife vitality (and grace), she left her husband, formed new relationships with her now-grown children, started a new career, and entered a new and healthier relationship with a man. She felt she had given birth to a new self and had a new lease on life—and she was right.

Then she had a dream, stunning in its details, that repeated itself four separate times during the week between our sessions, each time waking her in the dark hours before dawn. In the dream, she found herself in the old familiar melancholy of the home where she had lived with her former husband for over two decades, and she was keeping house for him, even though they both knew they were divorced. She finished her housework, then hesitated for a moment, because she knew what was coming next. Slowly she entered the bedroom and numbly got into the bed with her former husband. He looked at her and smirked knowingly.

These dreams, we realized, were letting her know in a dramatic way that, in the excitement of her new life, she was trying to act as if her old life never existed. Such a response is very human but it's also one-sided. Her psyche was reminding her that this naïve attitude was keeping her trapped in her old passive and depressing frame of mind. While this situation was continuing, she was losing touch with the strength, tenacity, and vitality she had shown in surviving and growing to new levels.

As she and I struggled toward a more balanced awareness, her vitality was slowly renewed. If she'd simply cut off the old, she would have lived with a deep and perhaps unconscious fear of repeating it. By integrating it, she was able to lose that anxiety.

People who simply want to leave their past behind them and get on with their lives (no matter how terrible their past has been) end up without an inner homeland. Instead, we must see that while each boundary crossing takes us to new places, all of them are still within our same psychic country. Thus, with a little insight, we can figure out our own heroic cycles, recognizing the periods of withdrawal, examination, turmoil, and discovery. Then we can return to our life in a renewed state of existence.

It is commonplace today to deny our fear of life and growth, but the old storytellers and priests knew better. They knew we are naturally afraid of every major threshold we have to cross, which is why they placed ferocious-appearing monsters at temple gates, covered cathedrals with gargoyles, and, with assorted monsters, guarded the rivers that must be crossed in mythological journeys.

These traditions remind us that we need courage and thoughtful preparation for our transitions. These images remind us that we fear life and growth at least as deeply as we desire them. Those fears are the reason behind the massive amount of self-help material on transitions that frequently clutter our bookshelves. But most of these self-help books don't help, because they are so focused on the process of getting through transitions painlessly that they ignore what the transitions mean, and so the character and the renewed vitality we could find in such experiences remain beyond our grasp.

Conventions as Boundaries

If we keep working to understand ourselves, we eventually become aware of the role that *conventions* play in our lives. Conventions are often either boundaries we must cross in our journey or walls that try to keep us within the boundaries. Many of these conventions were imposed on and adopted by us when we were children, long before our cognitive ability was mature. These conventions are nevertheless now a part of our personality—they live in our body, emotions and unconscious—because we weren't developed enough to be consciously aware of them, or if we were aware of them, we didn't know we had a choice when we accepted them. As we grow, however, we start to become aware of them and more knowledgeable about our choices. Then we must face these conventions and decide whether we want to accept or reject them. Thus, we can change them from externally-imposed conventions to self-imposed conventions if we value them and want to retain them.

Occasionally, when we refuse to recognize that these conventions are part of our psychology, nature provides a hidden teacher— through our body. For example, a man who was in analysis with me suddenly became sick for a number of days. Since his health was normally robust, we began to explore what the illness meant. The easiest answer would have been to say his marriage was toxic, but that wasn't news. He was, in fact, already contemplating divorce.

Eventually, we followed a path back into the mist of his origins. He had grown up in a family and in a religion that idealized marriage. Even though his present friends and minister supported his plans for divorce, the very idea of divorce literally made him sick. Through careful analytic work he realized that his unconscious "ideal" of marriage was keeping him in a destructive situation. His next task was to "divorce" this ideal and turn it into a self-imposed convention that he could consciously relate to...and, in this case, reject.

We need to be married to other human beings, not to concepts, conventions, or ideals. It is also helpful if the marriage is supported by a sense of love and commitment greater than mere personal attraction. In many cases this container may be strengthened by conventions during turbulent times, but we must be careful that we do not become trapped by those conventions.

Many of the conventions we adopted earlier in life served useful principles. They guided us into the world and gave purpose to our life. To suddenly reject them all would be a mistake. But we should ask ourselves how and where these conventions support us in the way we think and live today, and where they do us harm. The insight we gain by answering that question connects us to the life we are now living, as we become aware of which conventions are also boundaries. We may not like these discoveries and may even shrink from the entire process of self-examination. But, like it or not, we are responsible for the conventions we live by, and we must recognize that the choices we make now lay the groundwork for our future.

I am reminded of a middle-aged man who was considering a change in his life that could have reduced his income. At about that time, he dreamed he was in the ocean with his seventeen-year-old son and his own father. His son was holding onto one of his arms and his father to the other. They both were swimming deeper and deeper, pulling him down. As they descended, he was seized with panic because he was drowning and couldn't make them realize it.

After telling me the dream he observed that his son was applying to college and expected him to pay for it. As the man continued to deliberate these images with me, we realized that he had raised his son with the convention, which they both accepted, that paying for an education is a father's obligation. And the man's father had lived his life in conformity to the duties and obligations that were defined by his family and his church. With continued reflection, the man recognized that both figures in the dream symbolized obligations and responsibilities that were "drowning" him. A new door began to open with regard to his perspectives and he was able to consider fresh alternatives.

By continuing to pursue insight, we come to understand that we, to some extent, create the world we perceive because we view the world through the lens of our own psychological development. For one person the world may seem to be a threatening place; for another it may seem an expression of the Creator's love. We might think the world is the same in both cases and what's different are the two perceptions. However, we might also consider that the world is *not* the same in both cases, but is whatever each perceives it to be. More often than not, our perceptions help set up a model that the world and especially other people follow as they respond to us.

As our awareness of life grows, we begin to see the *ambivalences* that exist all around us. One person may follow all of the obligations of his or her religion while another does not. We know that one person may be blessed with good fortune while another is not. With this awareness, we set in motion a process that leads us to see that our relationships, including the one we have with ourselves, are also ambivalent. Unfortunately, we can't resolve many of life's ambiguities by simply changing or broadening our perceptions. We have to accept the fact that life is much more complex and unstable than we like to believe.

Denial and Choice

An awareness of life's ambiguities and complexities may lead us to a startling discovery. The journey through life that once felt well-grounded and stable in terms of our roles, beliefs, and conventions may now seem potentially turbulent, unstable, and beyond our control.

As we begin to experience more of life's changes and to question conventions, we find that the identity we built through all the struggles of adolescence and young adulthood—whether that of solid citizen or troublemaking rebel—is not as secure as we hoped it would be. In fact, the journey may begin to feel less like a solid trek over land and more like the voyage of a ship on a turbulent sea. Maybe we've recently run aground on one of life's shoals or feel as though we're caught in a squall we had not expected. Perhaps we are simply beginning to catch a glimmer that beneath our "solid" deck and hull lies an unfathomable deep, with creatures and currents we can't imagine.

Yet, we still long for peace, for affirmation, for direction. In searching for it, some people may have an affair, a middle-age crisis, or an emotional or physical breakdown. Others may batten down the hatches, covering their bodies with comforting carbohydrates. Still others may begin to jog compulsively around the deck or search for cures among the profusion of popular, oversimplified, "cure-yourself-in-a-weekend" distortions of legitimate medicine, psychology, or religion. All of these choices involve denying what we've seen of the depth and strength of the currents beneath us and, in the end, they rigidify our soul. These defensive tactics are the best many people can do, and I don't criticize anyone for drawing in and seeking security. In fact, I often envy those who seem to do so successfully—they may become bastions of the status quo, though they don't all have to become "old" and "bitter." However, my clinical experience has taught me to have a few reservations about the mental health of their children.

Others of us may choose to stay on deck. We still struggle to captain our little ship, searching for stars to guide us, for fair winds and compasses. At some profound level we realize this experience is not an illness. There is no cure. This is life. With that realization we must sail on, not out of courage (although courage is required), but because we realize we have no other choice.

Peace and Religion

As soon as we realize the ambivalent nature of life and the world, our inner social peace, the Pax Romana, quickly vanishes because we have learned that the conventional values and beliefs that helped us form our personality can only support a provisional life. But our longing for peace in the midst of threatening ambivalence has nevertheless always been a concern of the great religions. And, in the past few decades, searching for peace through religious rituals has become popular. (In many instances these rituals are more appealing when they're from other cultures, often out of context.) At the same time a growing number of people are trying to cling to certainty by becoming fundamentalists in whatever sect they find attractive, whether it's from their own culture or another. Both paths can lead to an illusory peace, but only at the cost of a denial of life.

These people are searching for peace through spiritual practices and the observance of religious principles that are not necessarily bad in themselves. At times, these practices and principles may, in fact, lead to a deeper spirituality. But one must be careful, because they can also lead to either an illusion of transcendence or dogmatic rigidity. Further, the attempt to transcend life and to create a bastion of spiritual virtue both deny the transformational journey.

War, conflict, and religion have had a curious relationship over the ages. Joseph Campbell observed that throughout history, societies reconciled to the hard nature of life and "bred to the mythologies of war" survived the best. In the Greek tradition *love* (symbolized by Aphrodite) and *war* (symbolized by Aries) were lovers. In the traditions emanating from the Old Testament, war and religion seem to be the two sides of the same coin. (The Old Testament idea of wars fought for Yahweh is as real as the Islamic notion of an unrelenting war in Allah's name.) Various paradoxical messages of Christ—such as "love your enemies and pray for those who persecute you" and "do not suppose that I have come to bring peace to the earth; I did not come to bring peace, but a sword"—seem to offer both a gospel of peace and a gospel of war when viewed literally. (For a number of centuries, Christians have gone gladly to war in Christ's name.)

In the East, Campbell noted as he sampled Eastern religious mythology, the Jain sect provides an example of a sort of fundamentalism for peace. Early Buddhist teachings reflected the Jain's desire to avoid rebirth into this dreadful world. Practitioners could avoid reincarnation by following strict rules of nonviolence and by having no personal desire to live. Buddhism led toward a quenching of the sense of "I" and "mine" and, according to Campbell, "…may lead ultimately to something very much like an absolute denial of life."[1] Another Eastern approach to peace centered around the teachings of Lao-tzu and Confucius, who taught that there "...is through all nature an all-suffusing spiritual harmony." Peace comes through aligning oneself with this harmony, in both an inner and outer sense.

Many Westerners who try to find peace through new-age spiritual techniques run into trouble when these techniques are taken out of their ground in the cultural wisdom and traditions of millennia. A few years ago, a friend of mine, an energetic executive, decided he needed to lower his general tension level. He was overweight, out of breath, and realized he was a heart attack waiting to happen. He began reading Zen literature, practicing yoga breathing exercises, and meditating on a regular basis. He lost weight and felt better. In fact, he discovered that he could work more efficiently, get more done. He increased his program until he was practicing and meditating in the office and even in airplanes so he could land refreshed and ready to work. He had his third heart attack and triple bypass surgery by age fifty.

His problem was that the techniques he was practicing were simply that—*techniques*. They had no spiritual meaning to him; they failed to connect him to anything deeper within himself. He lacked a traditional container for these techniques that had evolved through long human experience and that could truly connect him to his deeper or spiritual self. Which is not to say they couldn't have. But if they do, it requires an intense attitude of religious devotion and an understanding that goes beyond the mere practice of techniques and a feeling of relaxation and catharsis. He thought his practices were connecting him to the "light" and "transcendence," but these terms are really illusory, abstract, and far distant from a concrete, personal spirituality and may easily be diverted to support a sense of ego-inflation. As a result, his practices began to serve his driven ambition rather than his soul and, in the end, contributed to his physical deterioration.

---

1   Joseph Campbell, *Myths to Live By* (New York: Viking, 1972), 174-206.

In a similar vein, many Western students of Indian philosophy frequently miss the point of the *Bhagavad-Gita*, which they consider to be a spiritual work, is part of one of the greatest war epics of that region: the *Mahabharata*, or "Book of the Great War of the Sons of Bharata." This epic is awash in the ideas that "might is above right." Campbell sums up the ultimate ground in Oriental thinking as being that there is no peace and never will be in the field of human life.

Many religions, both Eastern and Western, take an apocalyptic point of view that peace on earth will result only from some great, final war between good and evil, when the powers of darkness are overthrown by the forces of peace and justice. Here we face the paradox that peace ultimately only results from conflict. The lives of the Western saints point to the same conclusions—their examples often lead us straight into the conflicts of life and even into conflict with God rather than to peace.

So in the end, religion does not offer us an easy way out as we approach a boundary crossing, though it may help us deny the crossing in an uncritical manner. But often an encounter with religion and spirituality is in itself a boundary crossing. As we re-encounter religion and spirituality in mature adulthood (or perhaps encounter it for the first time), we may find that our religion has a frightening depth we did not recognize earlier. We may also discover that our priest, minister, rabbi, or other spiritual leader is just another struggling human being who is as confused and lost as we are, and with as few answers. In many instances, letting go of our notion of God is the first step in letting go of our notions of ourselves, but many people in our modern age first have to *remember* forgotten ideas of God or even develop ideas of God from virtually nothing before they have something to let go of. Their search for self is often tied to a search for God that drives them to one after another of the pseudo-spiritual paths available today, or to have the naïve idealizations of nature and primitive peoples.

The search for God is not easy, for we who have either ignored traditions or have left them behind are missing the accumulated wisdom that lived in the great religions and long guided humanity through troubled spiritual waters. We are each left with an individual spiritual struggle to face, and for us to think we can avoid it is an illusion. If we subscribe to this illusion, then we pass the struggle on to the next generation, where we can see our failure reflected in promiscuity, drugs, and cults.

Boundaries and Choices

Our travels through life will bring us to many boundary situations. Often the boundaries will seem as natural and as appropriate to our development as the passage from childhood to adolescence or from adolescence to adulthood. Some boundary situations, such as accidents, illnesses, or deaths of those we love, seem utterly inappropriate, appear cruel, and are beyond our understanding. Yet others, like marriage or the birth of a child, will seem joyful. They are all crossings nonetheless.

Each of these events, whether internal or external, confronts us with a choice. We can decline to embrace life, usually by refusing to acknowledge what's happening or using the resources of medicine, psychology, or religion in an attempt to return to "normal."

I once knew a very active man who had a heart attack on the golf course. He was rushed to the hospital by his friends and barely saved. They were all severely shaken. But with the help of medical technology and doctors' platitudes, he was back to "normal" in a couple of weeks, and all who were involved continued living as if nothing had happened. He, and also his friends, had missed a *call*.

The other choice when we are confronted with a boundary crossing is to embrace life. This choice means accepting the processes of life, whether they are joyful, sorrowful, frightening, or simply tedious (as they may seem when our vitality withdraws from the world to answer an inner call to growth). To accept life this way, to embrace the impending conflicts and changes, is to do as Christ did when he, in St. Augustine's words, went to the cross as the bride and groom. Such an engagement of life lets us become participants in the creation of our character.

If we can pass through the fires of transformation, our life and personality will, like the Phoenix, rise anew with spirit and vitality. However, that Phoenix is not a totally new bird; it is a bird that has been transformed. It is new but at the same time constituted from the old. We are still who we are, but we will never be the same again.

PART TWO

THE TRUE GOLD

If you bring forth what is within you, what you bring forth will save you. If you do not bring forth what is within you, what you do not bring forth will destroy you.

— JESUS, *THE GOSPEL OF THOMAS*

Eros is a Kosmogonos, *a creator and father-mother of all higher consciousness... In my medical experience as well as my own life I have again and again been faced with the mystery of love, and have never been able to explain what it is... Here is the greatest and the smallest, the remotest and nearest, the highest and lowest, and we cannot discuss one side of it without also discussing the other. No language is adequate to this paradox. Whatever one can say, no words express the whole. To speak of partial aspects is always too much or too little, for only the whole is meaningful...For we are in the deepest sense the victims and the instruments of cosmogonic "love."*

— C.G. JUNG, *MEMORIES, DREAMS, REFLECTIONS*, PP. 353-354

Chapter 5

MIDLIFE—SHIFTING SHADOWS

Self-knowledge

Midday is a suitable analog for our psychological encounter with midlife. The symbolic sun of our personality is at its highest point and at this time the identity we have built is often at its pinnacle as well. Then, as the sun starts to move past its zenith and toward the horizon, we find that the shadows begin to shift and lengthen. Likewise, within ourselves we may sense the shifting of our inner perspectives.

Approaching any boundary situation in our psychological growth unbalances our energy. As we discussed in the previous chapter, the midday situation becomes even more unbalanced as we realize, even if only vaguely, that our life is neither what we think it is nor what we think it should be. This curious discovery may seem elusive, provocative, or even challenging. It may be humbling or terrifying. As all of this is happening, we also begin to catch glimpses of remote psychological realities that haunt us more than we have ever expected they might.

Our dreams may begin forewarning us. We may dream of living in a house that turns out to be an apartment or a dormitory, showing us that our personality is now in a transitional state. Or we may open a door and discover a hidden portal to some unknown place, warning us even further that we are about to make a passage. Perhaps it will lead into a mansion or a cathedral, or we may fall into a dusky basement or find ourselves in an open space with no shelter at all—an indication that the future is unclear and may be filled with promise or danger.

At this stage, when we are walking in the quiet, we may develop a vague sense that we are being followed. Perhaps, when we enter periods of contemplation (or, more likely in today's world, when fatigue overtakes us), we sense another presence moving along behind us. Unfamiliar figures may appear in our imagination or in our dreams, seeming ambivalent, even when they are pictured as friends, foes, robbers, or murderers. These figures usually leave us uncomfortable and afraid because we cannot truly tell if they want to help or harm us. They may represent our greatest fear, like the shadowy angel following Christ in *The Last Temptation of Christ*, Nikos Kazantzakis' powerful story of Christ's struggle to recognize and accept his identity and its ensuing destiny. We may fear the potentials of our own destiny, of living authentically, and worry that doing so might upset the life we've built.

These mysterious dream figures are the faces of our "shadow." You may recall that as we form our personality, the characteristics, attitudes, and ideals we have "chosen" are in the foreground of our self-consciousness. We present them to the world through our social personality or "persona." But the traits we have rejected have not disappeared. They have simply remained more or less in the background of our personality. This shadow is thus the reflection of a portion of our wholeness. If we deny or repress it, as we normally try to do, we become increasingly one-sided and lacking in human substances.

At the noon-point in our lives, when the light of our psychological sun shifts and begins its descent toward sunset, the time has come for us to go through a similar shift. We must start to direct our energies away from the creation of form and toward the loosening of form. This will allow us to reorient ourselves toward wholeness and prepare for the completion of our journey. Jung was fond of noting, "When *Yang* has reached its greatest strength, the dark power of *Yin* is born within its depths, for the night begins at midday."

When we face this transition, we can resist nature and struggle to keep building onto our hard-won form, but doing so is risky, and nature may tear us away from that form using such apparently uninvited problems as obesity, depression, panic attacks, chronic fatigue syndrome, or other malady, often one that seems beyond the understanding of medical science. This time of transition is especially precarious in an action-oriented society, which is so focused on moving ahead that we run right over our wake-up calls and transition periods, never realizing what we are doing until nature strikes us with a bolt from the blue.

The obsession with performance and the need for control seem to team up to create another danger in our societal selves—an idolizing of "identity." Identity in our media-based culture rests on recognition and power, and is generally based on controlling the impression we make on the public, even when the "public" consists of those we love. (As you might imagine, relationships, inner and outer, suffer when we over-focus on identity.) One of the greatest fears triggered by the noontime shift in perspective is the loss of control and the perceived public shame that may result. The cliché of the man who leaves his wife and family for a younger woman, his own apartment, and a sports car reflects one common reaction to this fear of the loss of control and the shame that often results from being judged and misunderstood by families, friends, and colleagues.

Without a doubt, our identity is legitimately threatened at mid-life, for it must change. It may loosen, rigidify, or transform, but it will not remain static. Fear may compel us to rush from our prior identity into an idealized new one, as many middle-aged women did in the seventies when they left their husbands and families and rushed into a new social identity that wasn't necessarily authentic. In such a case, we may appear to be fashionably self-actualized, but we may also live to discover that underneath the new identity, the old one still is present. We recognize that we have not made the transition until we come to grips with ourselves on the inner level as well. We simply cannot rush through this transition, because we need to discover too much about ourselves and life if we are to make it successfully.

Millennia of wisdom have taught that self-knowledge is the key to loosening our attachment to the form that is our identity. And a fundamental aspect of self-knowledge is figuring out how we assemble our picture of the world. Early in his career, Jung explored the various ways we do this. One of them involves what he called *psychological types*, which are important foundation stones in our development of form. In Jungian psychology, investigating these styles, or types, is a primary step in self-understanding, because the types we have chosen to incorporate into our personality play a large part in determining our perspective on life and how we relate to ourselves and others. Also, the opposites we rejected follow close behind us, causing us no end of problems until we assimilate them into that perspective.

In the fun of classifying ourselves and others, we often forget that Jung's essential message is that we should try to understand psychological types so we can better understand ourselves and become more open to the other types, both inside and outside of ourselves. These insights are some of the easiest we can come by as we begin a process of introspection.

Jung's primary classification of people into introverts and extroverts is well-known and widely accepted. Introverts prefer to focus their energy toward the inner world and extroverts toward the outer world. Our highly extroverted society makes life particularly uncomfortable for the introverts among us, but if we put the social ideal aside, we can see that both types, if they are to become better balanced and fulfilled, need to devote some energy to their opposite characteristics. In everyday life, the worst thing that can happen to an extrovert is to be excluded from a group, while the worst thing to an introvert is to be dominated by a group. But a time comes in our development when we should face such fears and, at that time, our dreams will picture our denied extroversion or introversion seeking to contact us. In dreams, the extrovert may find he or she is being pursued by a hermit and the introvert by a public speaker of some kind. These inner companions are a challenge at first, but eventually they will bring balance to the lives of both types.

After he developed the introvert/extrovert classification, Jung's curiosity carried him on to examine how we gather information and make decisions. He eventually worked out two sets of bipolar continuums, which he called the *psychological functions*, that describe the four aspects of reality he considered most important. The first set, *sensation* and *intuition*, deals with how we gather information. Sensation seeks out concrete, specific facts, while intuition looks at patterns and relationships. The second set, *thinking* and *feeling*, deals with how we make decisions. Thinking describes an objective process whereby we make decisions based on whether something is true or false. Feeling evaluates things as good or bad based on a personal value system.

In less technical terms, we might say that sensing reflects how a literal-minded, practical person views things and sizes up a situation. Intuition is how a person who prefers to understand possibilities functions and seeks to grasp the principles of things. Thinking may be what a scientist does, taking something apart to analyze it. Feeling may belong to an artist, who puts things together in original combinations. Of course, you can see that while these descriptions reflect preferences, none of them is clear-cut and able to stand on its own. They all require each other. Perhaps people of wisdom operate by combining and balancing them in order to fashion their picture of the world.

By the time we reach late adolescence, most of us have developed one of these four functions as the foundation for our approach to life. We usually augment the one we choose with a second selection, generally one from the other pair of functions. This second selection operates a little less consciously than the first, while the remaining two functions remain unconscious or comparatively undeveloped. Thus, we may have the fabled absent-minded professor, long on intuition and thinking and short on sensing and feeling.

An everyday example, such as the decision to buy a car, can further illustrate these points. A thinking type of person may approach this decision by conducting a financial analysis. This person is interested in the economics of the decision—cost, resale value, maintenance expenses, and other things affecting the "bottom line." Such a person may carefully research consumer bulletins and reports. A sensation type may be interested in how the car drives. Such a person will be interested in acceleration, cornering, and braking, and will study motor magazines. An intuitive type may be more interested in the possibilities the car provides and fantasize about trips and adventures or the ease of getting places. A feeling type may buy a car because the name, the style, the color, or the feel of the upholstery is appealing. All four processes are equally valid, though very different contents and styles of consciousness are involved. We might also imagine that combining all four of these processes could result in a more balanced and effective decision.

If we carry these notions a step further, to a collective level, we see that our society appreciates and rewards a style that is outgoing (extroverted), factual (sensing), and logical (thinking). Our media and institutions uphold as models people who appear practical, materially successful, have positive attitudes, make things happen, and seem in rational control of their lives. Values of the inner life—which are more subjective, creative, or spiritual—seem to be virtually ignored in our collective perspective.

From the foregoing assumption, we might speculate that as a society we frequently search for vision (intuition) and inspiration (personal, feeling values) in our leaders. We search for the qualities we are missing, looking for a leader who can outline a vision based on feeling values, one who will challenge us to a commitment, in the way we believe John F. Kennedy challenged us. But if we are looking for attributes that compensate for our collectively chosen style—meaning they are not our dominate values—we will have trouble sustaining them because they're not consciously integrated into our societal personality. (After all, Kennedy was elected by only the slimmest of margins.) We might also speculate that because we as a society have a poorly developed feeling function, we often have a limited range of, or inappropriate, feeling responses—

such as when we are excessively emotional, overly intense, and often unrealistically sentimental in our reactions to events. This line of thinking is validated by our recognizing how easily we become polarized to the point of being incapacitated over ticklish political issues. Our polarization and the ensuing frenzy point out that we have lost our orientation, which needs to be grounded in *thinking* and *feeling*, and have adopted overly rigid and overly emotional positions that reflect a loss of consciousness, balance, and maturity.

Back on a personal level, our first realization that these dichotomies genuinely exist may occur when we discover that someone close to us actually does think in a totally different way than we do. Then, if we begin looking into ourselves a little, we may realize that the preferences we structured into our personality were the result of adaptation to circumstances rather than truly authentic choices. For example, if we adapt well in school we will strive to fulfill societal norms, even if being something else is more natural for us. I've known many people who are introverts, intuitive and feelings types who struggled to fit in at home and at school by repressing their own preferences and trying to be someone they truly couldn't be. Whether they succeeded or failed in their efforts, the effects were often the same—they simply felt "different" and incapable of fitting in. We may also find our preferences changing over time, and the effects of these changes may be the source of both joy and trouble.

As useful as these realizations about others and our society may be, we should ultimately try to understand psychological types so we can better understand our own makeup. Furthermore, while typology can be very useful in developing communications skills, we miss the point if we allow the types to simply reduced to a handy classification system. They are keys to the front gate at the beginning of the path that leads to our interior.

Even as an initial exploration, this short examination of our styles of consciousness can be disturbing. If we take the types seriously, we can begin to see that the form of our personality, what brought order and direction to our life, is simply an illusion, created by ourselves and our group. Once we discover that we (and the influences we adapted to) created our identity, we may be startled or even terrified to realize it is like a dream and we are not sure what it really is or exactly how it was created. (One might argue that biology also has something to do with our form. While that's true, biology alone leaves the picture of who we are incomplete. In a similar fashion, dreams are also a function of biology on some level, yet they are both ever-changing and of deep psychological significance. Once we have begun to open the eye of self-consciousness, we find that, biology or not, we are always in process and cannot be fixed in form.)

As we face an awareness of the mutability of our form, we may encounter the deep injunction "look no farther"—or as it appears in many fairy tales, "do not open that door." But as the tales also reflect, some of us will always open the forbidden door. *Seeking* is a part of human nature and, sooner or later, we find that the order of life will not be denied and the great unknown marches inevitably toward us. The future remains undiscovered within us, awaiting an approaching birth that is forecasted in the never-ending flow of images we call dreams and fantasies.

Nevertheless, at the midpoint of our journey, our social personality may have become enough of a reality to entrap us and alienate us from ourselves and others. An understanding of this phenomenon, whether related to age or not, has been long and widely available and is even embedded in culture. Thus, for centuries the beautifully creative masks worn during carnivals in Europe were reminders that, if we get attached to our daily persona, we become caricatures of ourselves. Carnival masks released people from this bondage by allowing them to laugh at themselves in a yearly celebration. Laughing at ourselves and how seriously we pursue our daily roles is an art we have forgotten as a culture. The carnival celebrations were also connected to Lent, the approaching period of spiritual renewal in the Christian tradition. But we have failed to recognize the deeper meanings of both laughter and spiritual renewal and that a satisfactory human life demands more than Freud's old friends, love, and work. It demands *spirituality* and *laughter* as well.

Homo-duplex

Loren Eiseley, who penetrated science with the eyes of a poet, used the phrase *Homo-duplex* to describe creatures composed of both flesh and spirit. We do spring from nature, but we also contain an otherness, something that separates us from the rest of nature and the security of a life lived by pure instinct. This fall from nature into knowledge has left us in a state of both terror and wonder. The existentialists say we are in a state of basic anxiety, which we often seek to control by either knowledge or worship. But this view over-objectifies our situation. It may be more true to say that we are born into a state of mistrust that fuels our eternal search for meaning, which may turn out to be our greatest glory.

We are the only species with this idiosyncratic kind of consciousness, one that can comprehend all we were, all we have failed to be, and all we may become. We alone are the species that can add aesthetics to our lives, giving depth, comedy, tragedy, catharsis, and beauty—as well as horror—to the drama we are playing out. We continue to hold a basic fear of nature, of a chaos we can neither control nor feel at home in. Freud opened up the caverns of our own internal chaos and we are still afraid of what we see, even in the small light he was able to kindle. Right or wrong, we are afraid to look within—and that, too, is our nature.

Thus, we are always split. Nature follows the archetypal path of transformation: life, death, and rebirth. Jung, paraphrasing Goethe, described the path as one of, "Formation, transformation, Eternal Mind's eternal recreation," and Hegel intellectualized this process into thesis, antithesis, and synthesis. But feeling/thinking humanity experiences this natural process as punishment, torment, death, and transfiguration—and fears it. No wonder the Jains wanted to escape from the world. No wonder psychologists and psychiatrists, in a desperate grasp for something safe and controllable, describe our problems as behavior disorders and deny that we should feel bad. Escape, however, is not an answer, and we must go on in an effort to deepen our understanding of ourselves.

Dual Consciousness

Consciousness, following the pattern of our dual nature, may also be thought of as having two forms. In an effort to understand these complex and often contradictory attributes, analytical psychologists have classified them as *logos* and *eros*. Jung used the same terms to describe what he considered to be the masculine and feminine principles, respectively. The somewhat confusing fact is that these principles, as they are used in Jungian psychology, have little to do with gender or gender roles and a lot to do with all of us at deeper levels. Nevertheless, we need to understand these principles within ourselves as they are the foundation of the two fundamental ways we relate to each other and to nature.

Eros, as a psychological principle of consciousness, may be considered a receptive and holistic approach to existence as we participate in it. As we grow, eros begins with a sense of our dependence on being nurtured and, if this need is adequately met, evolves into loving desire for another and matures into compassion and wisdom. We access eros mostly through *reflection* and by being open to the events and experiences of our life. Logos, as a psychological principle of consciousness, on the other hand may be thought of as approaching life through our rational mind. Logos shines the light of intellect and intuition sharply into a situation as though from the standpoint of an observer. Logos begins with a sense of strength and separation. As we grow, it strives to initiate change and to develop knowledge, planning, and intellectual capacities. It brings meaning, clarity, order, and individual identity to the object of its focus. We get in touch with logos consciousness through insight and analysis, the careful examination of events and experiences of our lives. In the case of logos, self-understanding requires that we focus our own observing eye toward our interior.

Freud concluded that insight is the primary method for understanding ourselves. Jung agreed and always acknowledged his respect for Freud and his work in this area. But Jung took Freud's method-ology a step further by involving our imagination in a process of "in-sight into images." This term means to acknowledge that the images in our imagination, mind, fantasies, and dreams are psychologically real. Then we can examine them and, upon doing so, will find they have many useful meanings for us. Insight involves carefully exam-ining our interior life in a disciplined manner, seeking to understand it from a detached (though not impersonal) standpoint. Unfortu-nately, popular psychology, with its stages and steps of this and that, tends to skip across the depths of humanity like a stone thrown across the water, to gather a few labels or clever interpretations that might enable us to categorize ourselves or others. And, while these perfunctory classifications give the illusion of understanding, they are dangerous because they lead us far from our own truth.

Insight is an appropriate tool for developing self-knowledge during midlife. But, in order to find out who we really are, we must carry our "insight" into actual practice. If it doesn't affect the way we engage life, then it doesn't reflect self-knowledge at all. Thus, as we bring our insight into practice, we must make sure we keep our conscious eye open to watch the new interplay between the world within us and the one without. By doing so, we will invite new things, unexpected and unimagined things, into our experience, and our experiments in the art of living will build upon themselves. If our consciousness continues awakening during this time, we may find that our crusade for certainty gradually evolves into a search for understanding. This expanding awareness can lead us into what Jung called a process of "conscious individuation," a term to which we will return later.

Some time ago, I worked with a man who had been grappling with these issues for several years, ever since he suffered depression and vague feelings that he wasn't who he should be. His analytic work had been courageous and fruitful as he focused inward and became increasingly aware of aspects of himself deep in his psyche that he scarcely remembered. During much of this time he had been confused about the particular feelings he "thought" he should have and the things he "thought" he was supposed to do. By the time he had this dream, he had traveled far toward resolution.

"I dreamed that I was walking out of my childhood home, toward the garden," he said. "As I pass the corner of the house, I notice that I have two shadows. One is from the sun directly overhead, probably a little past noon. The other comes from the late-afternoon sun, setting in the west."

I sank back in my chair. "What do you think?"

He sighed, "I believe I may finally be leaving my childhood psychology. Interesting, isn't it, that I go through the back door and toward the garden."

"Gardens often symbolize feelings or new life," I said.

"But this was my father's garden. This was where he was most alive, an aliveness he could never have with people."

I waited in silence. His experience wasn't far from my own.

"I see my parents as people now," he said. "Small people, not big ones. Their power's gone and so is most of my hurt and rage. They did the best they could, given who they were. And I appreciate a lot of what they did. But they're just limited, fallible human beings."

"Yes," I replied. "I believe you're right. That's all they are and that's all we are." I knew this realization meant a lot to him because, as his parents became human, he was released from being the "good son," addicted to obligations—a much different state from that of consciously accepting responsibilities.

"Go on," I said. I like this kind of session, when an analysand moves beyond confusion and arrives at a deeper understanding.

"I was surprised at the two suns and the two shadows," he continued. "I've thought one shadow was enough to deal with. I suppose the first shadow is more my personal shadow, work I still have to do on myself. But the second one makes sense, too: the setting sun." He eyed me carefully. "You and I are both at the age where we become aware of death."

"I know." I sank a little lower into my chair. I was actually quite a bit older than he was.

He went on, realizing that he was in the process of crystallizing new insights about his earlier experiences and that these insights would change his life. This dream was a turning point in our work. A different future was now latent within him. Yet for all of the drama of his dream and the resulting insight, he still had not yet left the yard of his childhood home. And it was from within that yard that he was becoming more aware of death. Perhaps, I thought, his growing awareness of death would compel him to venture out and journey farther until he found the symbolic ground of his own life.

Morning and Noon—Passing Back and Forth

Long before he had his dream of the two suns, this man had begun to remember details of the foggy morning from which he emerged. Old childhood fears, terrors, and memories crept out of his inner caverns like sleepy dragons, as if to harry him a final time. Thus it is with all of us. If we are to resolve our inner story, we must be willing to travel from where we are now back to where we were in our past. Then we must follow an opposite process of returning to our present-day life. But we return with new insights into our own nature and therefore into our way of life, our values, and our religion (if we were raised in one). Passing back and forth from today's standpoint to yesterday's is a psychological adventure that brings us into relationship with our own life in an increasingly objective and yet also personal way. This process is a crucial part of our midday experience.

If we are fortunate enough to have adolescent children and have had the luck to stumble into some awareness of our own inner journey, we will find that curious events are taking place in the context of the relationship between our children and ourselves. Until this point, we may only have had a wispy sense of our own youth, the time we teetered on the edge of life, full of hope and fear. This youthful aspect yet lives within us as a ghost, part of our beginning and now part of the self we have become. And with an enhanced awareness of this aspect, we may see, in a new way, opportunities taken, missed, and never even noticed.

As our children become adolescents, all of the fundamental questions of life return to confront us because our children are facing them for the first time: "How do I live?" "Is there a meaning?" "What is life?" "Why am I here?" If we have the courage, we can renew our own struggle with these questions and share it with our children, both finding our own way and giving them the courage to find theirs. Or, we can flee into a fortress of convention, busyness, and practicality, letting our own ghost, repressed and turned sour, infect our children.

If we have begun to pay attention to ourselves, we soon become aware that our ascent into adulthood was both a pursuit and a flight. We were pursuing life and we were fleeing the things we dreaded, whether we were conscious of them or not. If we choose now to remain unconscious, we curse our children with our acknowledged needs and our regrets over opportunities we missed. If we don't do our own inner work, the unresolved and uninvestigated chapters in our own story become woven into theirs. This is a curse because we are supposed to give them life, not rob them of it. Their lives are not meant to fulfill our unmet needs and unrealized hopes, though the grace of their lives can remind us of the depth and importance of our own life.

Once again, dreams can be an inner teacher. I remember the dream of an austere man with a house full of adolescents. When the dream began he was in his office. Four tacky salesmen forced their way past his secretary and tried to sell him life insurance. The dream ended at this point.

To amplify his understanding, he decided to have a dialogue with an inner feminine figure from a previous dream (this is the technique I mentioned in the introduction). Helen, as he called her, had helped him figure himself out several times before.

"Helen," he said, "what do these guys mean anyway?"

"Oh, they're just a joke we're using to get your attention," Helen said. "No one can sell you life insurance."

"What?"

"You're the only one who can ensure your life has value and

meaning. No one can do that for you, and you certainly can't buy value and meaning, despite what society today says. You can't ensure your life by self-sacrifice and deprivation, either. That's just the other side of buying it."

Sometimes our dreaming self is less whimsical and more dramatic, using midnight images to bring us face-to-face with our midday questions. A woman I worked with once dreamed that she was speeding recklessly down the expressway in her silver BMW (which she owns, in fact). She pulled off into a good neighborhood of the city and reached a four-way stop. The street signs read north, south, east, and west. Suddenly she realized her car was filled with vampires and her door would not open.

When we discussed the dream, we discovered she had reached her midday crossroads. Her identity, won through years of scholarship, hard work, and professional achievement, had been too weak to sustain her for the last few years, but she was too "driven" to notice. The time had come for her to begin a careful search for the true gold of the Self and, through this search, develop a more full and enriching relationship with herself and her life, even though she had felt her life, as she was already living it, was sufficient.

The lesson in this dream is hard and frightening, but our rich and power-oriented way of getting around in the world may likewise become a tomb of horror, filled with vampires that entrap us. The vampires of an idealized lifestyle and success may seize us and seductively suck away our vitality while we think we are doing admirably.

Toward the Horizon

The shifting perspective we call human nature leaves us with only one true choice in life—to grow, to find the latency hidden within us, and to try to bring it into being. This is the destiny of humanity. If we try to preserve the self we've developed, we will soon become so obsessed with the task of preservation that, in reality, we end up losing our self, so only the shell of our form remains. Anxiety creeps in to fill our hollowness and shows itself through rigidity, dependence, and addictions, although we may appear to be quite solid. There is no compromise with the truth that we must be willing to "lose our life in order to find it."

Passing back and forth from our present to our past brings us into relationship with ourselves. It opens us to unexpected and unforeseen adventures, inner and outer. The insights we gain from revisiting our past help release the shadowy figures of lost essences and put us in touch with new ideas that reach inward to our hearts and minds, and forward to our destiny and happiness.

Once we have returned from the past, we bring to our lives a different ideal—a new, conscious attitude that will guide us. The difference between our new self and our old can seem small from the outside, but inside we may be powerfully transformed. Moreover, we will have discovered insight and the importance of transformation.

After midday, our call is to journey on. We may leave this period with the knowledge that the shell of the form we worked so hard to build lies cracked open like an egg. Perhaps something new has been born. And somewhere in our primeval, imaginal interior a snake—that ancient symbol of the necessary sin, transformation, and healing—may be slithering away, possibly smiling.

Chapter 6

PASSING MIDLIFE—CRITICAL MASS

In the Heat of Life

Often, especially in late summer, the intensity of the sun seems to increase after it has passed midday. The same is true with our experience of life. Passing the midlife boundary doesn't mean we are declining. In fact, the primary ingredients of growth—the heat and light of our lives—may be increasing. Our emotional intensity, the desire for self-knowledge, and a more fulfilling orientation toward living may be developing.

This early afternoon heat, which includes emotional intensification, may strike us like restlessness struck King Arthur's knights once their world had been tamed. In a manner similar to theirs, we may feel agitated and confused as the increasing heat of approaching and arriving midlife has begun to stir some of the content of our depths. Our "stuff," which has settled over the years, is becoming unsettled.

In their quest to find the meaning of life, the old alchemists taught that the stuff settling in the alchemical vessel (the symbolic container of life) needed to be heated in order to generate new life and to renew the course of transformation toward symbolic gold. To them, symbolic gold represented wholeness, the fulfillment of the pattern that lies within us with the potential to be fulfilled.

Once heated, the substance of a settled life may need careful distilling, since the alchemical heat stirred by life's early afternoon, as it bubbles through us, frequently is a product of the emotions we worked the hardest to regulate in our earlier development. The careful distillation of our bubbling interior can best come through insight. Insight follows the ageless decree of Apollo, the sun god, to bring balance to our life by turning inward and seeking self-knowledge. Apollo's influence, however, seems slowly to have withered in our imagination, as society appears bent on an endless quest for experience, with little desire for insight and even less for moderation.

In its early days, the practice of psychotherapy was founded on insight, but psychotherapists found this method difficult to sustain. Freud nevertheless opened a door to our interior, revealing a dimension formerly reserved for poets and prophets, endeavoring to bring the notions of religion and philosophy into the no-longer-sacred temple of Apollo in search for the truth of our lives. But the literal mind still has difficulty in the subterranean cosmos of our non-rational selves. Moreover, as we use a brighter light, the shadows often seem to become darker. Collectively, we have apparently become too easily frightened by these shadows. And we seem to long for simplistic models as ways of dealing with them— the comfort of cursory humanistic healers, the denial practiced by psychiatry when it substitutes taking drugs for healing, and the superficial labels and quick-fix techniques becoming popular in counseling and psychology. Facing our inner self with courage is becoming a forgotten art, and even beginning the search for our own truth is no easy task. Many of us will find it easier to blame somebody else for our troubles or look for an easy way around them.

But insight is difficult to forget once it has been tasted. One small bit of awareness leads us to seek another, and before we know it a journey is underway. Soon we realize that this bittersweet addiction is built into our nature, for we are born to be seekers. If we are also able to find a little courage (and life can help us find this courage through a feeling of desperation), we may begin to share our insight with someone else who is kind and understanding—and we may find that experience helpful. Initially, doing so can be painful, and we must proceed carefully until we are sure we can trust the other person and trust ourselves when we are with that person.

In ancient Greece, entering the temple of the sun god meant entering a sacred place. Very little space is sacred today, so we must somehow learn to construct or discover this space on our own. As we communicate our beginning insights to a special or gifted person, if we do so gently, we find out that we receive further insight in return, though it will rarely turn out to be what we expect. As we continue doing this, we begin to sense that some yet unknown destination is beckoning us. Immediately our modern minds will say there must be a "right" way to do this process. At such a point, we are in danger of replacing our quest for insight with a quest for methodology. Deeper insight into ourselves, however, may soon teach us to begin reserving our judgment. It will also dampen our tendency to turn from sharing insights, our inclination instead to make pronouncements and declare conclusions. As we journey farther, we slowly learn that neither "the way" nor "our way" is so easy to discern. We must then start to wonder if the way of insight is enough, or whether it is only a beginning. In truth, we discover, it is a beginning—an afternoon beginning.

Interior Sunlight

To search for insight into our relationship with ourselves and others is a symbolic descent, which mythology describes as a journey downward, often into hell. There is no easy way around this task. It requires courage; an acceptance of an unfolding, unknown destiny; honesty; and, as Dante points out, a guide. If we aren't careful, we will simply travel with the crowd, missing the appeal of the quiet voice within, and never even realize we are searching for a direction. We must learn to recognize our real nature and that, while this nature is the foundation of most of our problems, relationships, and successes, it is trying to *become*, trying to lead us into a fulfilling future.

We may begin our endeavor to look inward by having a discussion with ourselves. We can start with questions, self-examination, searching for the subterranean movements and hidden attitudes that have been influencing our perspective.

This questioning process can be very simple. Freud suggested that we begin by asking what things affect our feelings, thoughts, and actions in everyday activities. These are straightforward questions to enlarge our self-awareness. "Why did I forget that appointment?" Perhaps I feared the new demand on my time that might result. "Why did that brief comment cast me into a mood of depression?" Maybe it threatened some secret pride or unadmitted ambition. "Why did I get so angry at my spouse's (or lover's) remark?" Perhaps I am more dependent on his or her approval than I like to admit. "Why did I feel so hurt when my friend canceled our lunch date?" Do I feel rejected? At this point, we all hope to find admirable, hidden attributes in ourselves. And while we may find them, the wisdom of humanity's experiences teaches us that our reward is more likely to come from facing the shadows we wish to hide.

An example of this kind of work can be seen in an analytic hour in which I was participating a few years ago. In this case, a man well-established in his life was going to make a dramatic career move. His elderly parents were vigorously opposed to the move and, after a heated argument, were maintaining an uneasy truce.

As my discussion with the man proceeded, he said, "They're just too old to understand. Their standpoint is fixed and they are too far gone to change."

"It seems to me," I answered, "that you haven't really explained to them the real reasons for making this move. You make it sound like a holiday instead of a matter of your spiritual life or death. Nor have you pointed out that you are very intelligent, very successful, and that they need to show you more respect."

He laughed and said, "Oh, they don't believe any of this psychology stuff. The kindest thing for me to do is simply to go on my way as if nothing has happened, be nice to them on a surface level, and do what I want to do."

I worked with him for many hours, and a recent series of his dreams had led me to believe that the time had come to confront him about his parents and some of the hidden darkness in his attitude toward them. I said, "I don't think that is kind at all. I think it is the most passive-aggressive thing to do. If they weren't concerned, they wouldn't be arguing with you. To be honest, I think avoiding being direct allows you to keep your aloof position with them. It isn't kind, because it covers up how much you like to despise them."

Slowly his face began to flush, his eyes became intense, and he clasped his hands. A long silence followed. He relaxed his hands. "Damn it," he said, "you're right!"

In our interior descent, we soon encounter the shadow figures we earlier despised and discarded while we were selecting the supposedly more desirable attributes in our personality. To our amazement, however, we find that these disparate parts did not simply remain locked in some forgotten inner cellar. They have been around us all the time, returning again and again in the form of problems and of various other people in our lives—just as the man's problems with his parents had been around. We have been reading into other people and other situations much of what is, in fact, in ourselves. This awareness is not very flattering, and, having had it, we may feel stupid and vulnerable, but this comprehension begins the discovery of much that is valuable about our personality.

Of course, we can be irritated with or dislike someone without this antipathy being the result of our projecting[1] onto them the things we dislike about ourselves. However, if we want to know whether we *are* projecting, what can convince us is the emotional strength of our feelings and our inability to get rid of them.

Resentment, for example, is the emotional path that can lead us most directly into the knowledge that we need to take a look at

---

1   Projection is the psychological term for the unconscious displacement of our personal attributes onto other people or objects. The projected contents may be unacceptable emotions or qualities, or they may be beneficial and valuable ones. The recollection and integration of projected contents is an important part of Jungian analysis and any journey into self-understanding.

our shadow. Whenever we engage in one of those ongoing diatribes behind the wheel of our car or an angry inner conversation with an adversary keeps us awake into the dark hours, we are assuredly in the emotional web of a projection. A careful and courageous examination may help us understand how we act or feel the same way as does our antagonist. The man I just discussed acted as if his parents refused to understand him and treated him with disdain. In fact, though, he himself was setting this situation up as well as refusing to understand his parents and treating *them* with disdain.

Withdrawing projections is a slow and onerous task. Through painful and humiliating (as his analytic session demonstrated), this process also leads to a sense of inner peace as we come to feel more at home in ourselves and thereby in the world.

Once we begin this type of inner exploration, our dreams will furnish us with a flow of information about our "others." Same-sex figures in our dreams generally represent our shadow qualities. For example, a woman oriented toward social activism dreamed continually that she lived in the rich area of her town and was president of the country club. After a lengthy discussion of her dream with me, she realized that she had hidden her own desire for success and influence. And, furthermore, we uncovered how she had unconsciously excused the lack of ambition in herself as well as in her charming Peter Pan husband by projecting greed and shallowness onto the more affluent people in her area—people who, of course, she had refused to get to know. This insight does not mean she was a greedy, superficial person below the surface. It means that as she repressed her desire for a fuller, more complete life, aspects of that desire took primitive forms when they were repressed. In other words, when she repressed her ambition, all of the hallmarks of an ambitious person appeared negative in her one-sided perspective.

Similarly, a prominent man dreamed his blood was being sucked away by a group of zombie vampires. We slowly explored these images, along with the fantasies and emotions they evoked. A look of shock crossed his face as he concluded that most of his colleagues and many of his friends might see *him* as a bloodsucker.

He realized that most people probably did see him as such a creature and that his insecurity was killing the vitality in himself and in those around him. This insight led him to question the validity of the principles that governed his life—his own unconscious conventions.

Once we understand this process, the idea of praying for our enemies takes on an entirely different meaning because their stronghold lies within ourselves. A lovely story I once heard enlivens this idea. St. Peter was showing a new arrival around heaven. As they walked through the streets, the curious newcomer saw some people he had despised on Earth. He pointed them out and asked, "What are they doing here?" St. Peter answered, "Don't you remember? You prayed for them." The man, beginning to feel proud of himself and his power, replied, "You mean they are here because I prayed for them?" "No," St. Peter replied, "that's why *you* are here."

Gradually our awareness grows that dualism (Homo-duplex) is hidden in every crevice of our nature. In older times, good versus evil was the primary symbol of this division. Today, it seems to be form versus chaos. In fact, first man in his earliest cave drawings instinctively perceived a split in our perception of the forms of life. He drew an *elemental* form behind his idea of the everyday forms long before the rational mind of Plato imaged the cave. This ancient ancestor of ours, feeling that something inexpressible, numinous, and ominous was behind our experience—some invisible reality greater than the one we perceive—worshiped and worked in an effort to bring, through the greater expression of this reality, a little certainty to the world.

We haven't changed. We have the same relentless vision of something greater than our perception pursuing us, pursuing us from the depth of our unconscious, always seeking to break through the illusion of our ego-personality,[2] and frightening us in the silent

---

2   The ego is the symbolic sunlight of consciousness. In psychological terms, it is the center of our field of consciousness and gives us our sense of form, purpose, and identity. It organizes our conscious mind.

places of our lives. No wonder many of us fear the silence so much. One aspect of our deeper reality is that we are always in process and can never be fixed in form. The possibility that following the admonition "carpe diem" (seize the day) can provide satisfaction is an illusion, for the day—or even the moment, for that matter—can never be seized. The archetypal processes of transformation—the dynamics of life and its changes and endless renewals—are a psychological reality pleading for contemporary recognition in the psyche of humanity.

Heat

Often our heat is trapped deep inside us, as though it were in some underground volcanic canker. When this happens, we are psychically wounded. Somewhere down there we have a powerful rage, and perhaps a well of grief. In any event, our life force is trapped beneath the surface and has no opportunity to be lived. The following occurrence in the analysis of a woman shortly past midlife offers us a classic example of this sort of predicament.

She came quietly into my office at her regular time, handed me the copies of her dreams for my files, and began to cry. She began telling me her dream:

> I was walking back and forth between my childhood home and the house of my ex-husband. There was a forest in between. I was about eight or nine. My father came out of the woods, grabbed me, and dragged me in. Then he started doing the same things he always did when we were alone.

I sat quietly, giving her a box of tissues. I knew the situation from our earlier work. She continued:

> It was awful. I could feel the semen on my legs, gooey, sticky, horrible. Dear God, am I crazy? This happened so long ago. Haven't I dealt with it yet?

A voice in the back of my head, a feminine voice, said, "Be quiet. Listen. Listen. Don't jump in and try to fix it, explain the dream, or make her feel better." I obeyed. She went on:

> I tried to tell my mom once and he went crazy. He was drunk, as usual. He threw me on the bed, beating me with his belt. Mother threw her body on top of mine and he beat the living hell out of us. I never said another word.

She dissolved into sobs. "How do your honor your father? How do you forgive?" she asked.

I answered quietly, "You don't. I would hate him forever. He never asked for your forgiveness, did he? He never made a move toward reconciliation, did he?"

Forgiveness is never simple. Reconciliation and forgiveness can only come through atonement, a full taking of responsibility for what we have done or not done, and how that hurt someone. Without that, it's up to God. I would never have forgiven him anyway. I live better with myself when I am not trying to be a pious hypocrite, even though I have to struggle to be conscious of my own tendency in this direction.

We are taught, or so we think, that forgiveness is divine and that self-sacrificial love is the perfect manifestation of the divine will. These messages can feed our morning conclusions that we are powerless and must submit. When they are taken as a rule—perfunctory, simplistic, and meaningless—our soul is slowly murdered and we often learn, too young, to begin murdering our soul in order to maintain the illusion of peace and harmony in the family.

We learn to control our feelings, and somehow the notion that anger is always unhealthy and that good people are patient sufferers seem to support our efforts. We admire the idea of being in control of ourselves. But anger is important. It teaches us that we too have needs and it protects our boundaries, giving us inner space in which to live and grow. Anger keeps those away who want too much from us or who fail to treat us with dignity and respect.

Anger helps us define our values: what is worth getting angry about and fighting for?

Looking beneath or through the values of our early teachings can often help us break the bonds that trap our true feelings in a cage of fear. A middle-aged man experiencing such a trap came to see me at the suggestion of a friend. He related a terrible story from the misty beginning of his life. He was walking into his home with his mother, helping her carry the groceries in the way a three-year-old tries to help. As they walked up the front steps and into the house, they heard an explosion. His father had just put a shotgun barrel in his mouth and pulled the trigger.

He told me he had worked on this scene in therapy for several years before he began seeing me for analysis. He had cried and grieved. His former therapist had talked about compassion and forgiveness and about his father's horrible war experiences, even noting that perhaps the act of suicide was a gift from his father, an act that may have kept the man from going on to become a drunk and an abuser. The therapist tried, using conventional therapeutic approaches, to help the man come to a sense of peace and forgiveness. For over a year this approach had not worked. The man was still caught in that explosive moment and his frustrated therapist had referred him to me.

I sat back thoughtfully after hearing this story. The voice (feminine, of course) in the back of my head was there again: "You know what to say. Say it gently, quietly, carefully. You know the toughest things must be said quietly."

I said, "Is he buried near here?"

"Yes."

"I would go piss on his grave."

"What?" He looked very surprised, disconcerted, and almost angry.

"I would go piss on his grave."

A very long pause. "Maybe I will. I kind of like that idea…"

He did, and in our next session his analysis really began.

The points in these stories are not easy to read or digest.

Honoring our parents is, in the Judeo-Christian tradition, often understood as being required by God's law. Perhaps life is now trying to teach us that we must take this law a bit higher and separate it from our personal parents. We may need to honor our father and mother in heaven. Or, in other words, we might consider honoring those great archetypal images within ourselves that can bring about, nurture, protect, and guide our rebirth and continual transformation, if we can separate them from our actual parents. We initially project these images on our parents and thereby give our parents godlike powers. But we must reclaim these projections or we will forever remain "children," unable to initiate and foster our own psychological transformation.

Sometimes dealing with hate and rage is a paradoxical issue. The best way in some cases to avoid living a life filled with hate is simply to admit the hate, accept its reality, and ritually act to express it. The ritual act of pissing on the grave freed the man in my example from being possessed by rage and hate. This act brought peace of mind and the beginning of his personal journey out of the effects of his childhood trauma. Does he have to forgive his father? No. Can he hate him for the rest of his life? Yes. But now his hate will carry no disturbing effect; it won't possess him and thwart his ability to live.

In giving these examples I am not advocating that we become cursory iconoclasts. Inner work must be done carefully and thoughtfully, and we must be conscious of the ambivalence of our tasks. If rage or hate is destroying us, eating at our soul, we must learn how to come to terms with it. (If, however, it is not actually there, we don't need to conjure it up in some misguided attempt to work things through.) We must face our rage, hate, or grief, recognizing it as our wolf, and find the way to feed that wolf. In such a case, we may need healing and understanding, and we may need to learn how to give up our hate or transform it. On the other hand, we may need to learn that good, clean, old-fashioned hate can sometimes set us free from an emotional prison.

Jealousy and envy are two other powerful emotions that are part of nature's efforts to bring us to life and into transformation. These emotions are fundamental to being human. In today's climate, the useful and valuable traditions of self-actualization and humanism have often been reduced to simplistic concepts bolstered by catchwords like "empowerment" or phrases like "take control of your life." As our traditions become more utilitarian, more surface- and appearance-oriented, they deny the vitality of the ambivalent, irrational aspects of ourselves as strongly as did many of our childhood admonitions to "be nice" and "be good." To disown these parts of ourselves is to disown our emotional body and the fertile energy of our instinctual self. Our inner teacher can continue to guide us when we find ourselves not being, or even wanting to be, *nice* or *accepting*, and feel stuck in a conflict with conventional attitudes.

This discussion reminds me of another person I worked with. She was a very gentle woman, brought up to be *nice* and trained to be a humanistic therapist. During our work she began some inner dialogues and asked a dream figure (to whom she referred as Inanna) about herself and an impasse she was experiencing. She got this response: "Dare to connect to your instincts. They alone will save you. It is not mean to be real. It is not mean to be yourself. If there is a meanness in it, it will change as you see it. If it is seen, it moves—if not, it stays stuck. No movement means no life."

Anger, rage, resentment, envy, grief, and hate can all destroy us, especially if we are stuck in them. A straightforward experience of them (not to be confused with unconscious acting out) can often be a privileged moment of opening in our personality. These emotions represent some of the deepest forces of creation. The man pissing on his father's grave was carrying out a ritual enactment that opened the door to the next threshold in his psychic life as well as the door to the childhood that had imprisoned him. Paradoxically, this expression of hate became a moment of prayer, opening him to love and healing. His world was forever changed.

Another situation of this type, where things may not be as they first appear, comes to mind. I was giving a lecture on Jungian psychology when a man stood up and asked a question I often hear. "What about Toni Wolf?" (Toni Wolf was a close colleague and confidant of Jung, and their relationship has stimulated speculation as to its nature for years.) That feminine voice lurking in the back of my head began answering straight out of my mouth before I even realized it. I found myself saying, "Well, I always imagined that in those moments she was an angel."

She/I continued, "What do you think about the women in the life of Martin Luther King?"

The gentleman responded, "I don't know about them, but I think *he* was a great spiritual leader."

"And he was under a lot of stress and pressure."

"Of course."

She and I answered, "I agree. And can you imagine that those women may have been angels God sent to help him through those awful times?"

"No," he answered. "I wouldn't like to think that way."

"Well, let's continue what we were talking about," I said, thinking to myself that I had to keep a better eye on that feminine voice in me or she was going to get me in a lot of trouble someday. Nevertheless, as I continued the lecture, I had a brief inner image of a woman far back in a cave, smiling. A snake seemed to be back there, too. Was she petting it?

My intent is to emphasize the ambivalence of these emotions, their vitality, and our choices. We can live exclusively by the old code. We can live exclusively by the new fashion. Or we can choose to take from each what seems appropriate, to enter into the tension of every situation hoping to come out with a little more integrity and a little more clarity. The ambiguity, the duality, and the conflict increase along with our conscious awareness. Paradoxically, we may find ourselves emotionally crucified more often, although, curiously, life becomes less and less painful in a neurotic way, meaning the way we create pain for ourselves when we attempt to deny or repress the reality of our life.

In these stories, I have attempted to show how the foreground and the background of our so-called normal perspective need to shift as consciousness develops. This shift may occur to facilitate healing at any time, but it is also a specifically archetypal shift that needs to take place in the afternoon of life, when the foreground and the background of our shadows are already shifting anyway. Then it allows us to develop a broader perspective on life and a deeper understanding of ourselves.

Peace and Conflict in the Afternoon

The Old Testament idea of peace grew beyond the notion of simple outer tranquility by including the idea that relationships should be ordered and equitable. The beliefs, ideas, and resulting rules of conduct in that ancient time, as well as both social and religious relationships, illustrate the importance the Old Testament writings had in structuring the developmental form (identity) of that society. This cultural form defined the relationships among people and the relationship between people and God in what was considered to be an equitable and ordered manner. As that society's form continued through time, we might imagine that, in a psychological sense, its guiding structures of laws and rituals became increasingly hollow as they became habitual and entrenched. As this process occurred, we can also surmise that the deeper principles of relationship and equity were lost as they became increasingly systematized and institutionalized. Psychologically, the scene was then set for the transformative period that followed in the New Testament.

Again, this is the pattern of life. The form that evolved through struggle and suffering, filled with vitality, begins the process of stagnating, which will lead to future change. Either it must be revitalized on a new and higher level or it will wither and die in an eternal process that will bring forth something new in its place. We recognize, then, that peace is an interim condition, not a permanent state. The very placidity of peace leads to unrest and revolution as life continues on its transformative course. Paradoxically, peace in this perspective is pointing toward the future, and the only way to find peace is to release our current position and enter the struggle for either revitalization or new life. Seeking peace in a profound sense may be seeking completion, and in this respect cannot be static.

A similar process has gone on in our own development. The emotional heat of the afternoon returns us to the search for a renewal of relationship with, and equity with, the forces of instinctual life within us. This search, by its nature, demands an accompanying search for increased consciousness, as we have gained nothing if we simply allow ourselves to slide back into a "natural" state ruled solely by instincts.

At this point, we may begin to feel weary, somewhat like many of the Israelites did after fleeing Egypt. We are fatigued and we long for the old ways, the old attitudes, and the old consciousness in which we learned to feel secure. Some of us may actually return and stay there. But this old standpoint, though secure, enslaves and exploits us. In addition, returning to the old style sets the stage for more violent conflicts in both the world within and without, for it requires the assumption of a rigid and deadly defensiveness against the process of life. The symbolism of war in our inner world, often pictured in dreams or experienced in emotional or physical dis-eases, represents this struggle between our conscious ego and our unconscious, which threatens chaos.

Loren Eiseley has compared the development of life in general to a long war against a hostile environment. He notes:

> It began with strange chemicals seething under a sky lacking in oxygen; it was waged through long ages until the first green plants learned to harness the light of the nearest star, our sun. The human brain, so frail, so perishable, so full of inexhaustible dreams and hungers, burns by the power of the leaf.[3]

The alchemy of the afternoon leads us through the ambivalences of life by thrusting us into life's paradoxical nature. God may become the great iconoclast, smashing the idols and illusions

---

3   Loren Eiseley, *The Star Thrower* (New York: Harcourt Brace, 1978), 118.

upon which we depend. The mythic symbol of the crucifixion illustrates our suffering as we become conscious of the paradoxes of life and, at the same time, it symbolizes our path to wholeness and becomes the way to freedom.

A friend of mine, a fine physician and one of the most genuine people I know, followed the conventional path for well over forty years and had done so with care and intelligence. He told me the following story.

He was on call at his small community hospital when a fellow came in for treatment. Previously my friend had treated the man's wife and children. In this doctor's mind they had been severely abused (later the wife died in strange circumstances). Nothing could be proven and the wife refused to testify, but the little community remained suspicious of this obviously brutal man.

My friend, deeply Christian, began an inner struggle. He asked himself if he could treat the man, knowing no one else was available. He wondered how he could find the image of Christ, something to love, in this despicable person. He shared his dilemma with a colleague. His colleague answered, "Christ told you what to do. Remember when he said to Judas, 'do what you must.'"

After pondering this situation for a while, he later told me, "You know, I realized what a cursory, co-dependent kind of Christian love I've been trying to practice. This incident has really shaken me up. Things aren't so black-and-white anymore, nor is love so nicey-nicey. And I am pretty judgmental."

"I answered him, musing, "Do you see the image of Christ in that man now?"

"No, I'm still having trouble there," he replied.

"It seems to me," I conjectured, "that your encounter with him may have changed your entire perspective of Christianity. Transformed it. Maybe that's what Christ is—an image of transformation."

"I'm sure of that," he replied, "but it isn't so easy to figure out what that means. I've got a feeling I'm going to have to think about this one a long time."

The Long Shadow

In the previous chapter, I mentioned a dream with two shadows in it, with the second being from the setting sun, an image of our awareness of death becoming personal and explicit. Until midlife, barring unusual circumstances, death is something that happens to people, in general. Now we realize that it is going to happen to us, in particular.

Some of us have seen how emotional shocks—bolts from the blue—threaten and upset our psychic status quo and thereby have the potential to begin a transformative process. This realization about death is very special and difficult and can clearly be one of those "bolts." It may begin to make us more human. Hopefully it will lead us to deeper reflection (a subject in the next chapter), a more profound spiritual life, and an increasing concern for culture.

Life seems to be a battle against the dark, of consciousness against unconsciousness, which we have little chance of winning. The lethargy of our religious institutions and their focus on secular matters rather than on mysteries of life and death has left us feeling abandoned. We are alone in the face of our death, and this fact is a hard one. If we have the courage to face its reality, death will collapse our self-centered ideas, especially the idea that we can control our lives. Exclusively rational outlooks and pop-psych or pop-religious catchwords disintegrate in the face of death. The need for the inner journey and spirituality is awakened. Reflection is compelled because the Promethean fire of rational consciousness cannot light eternity and our insight cannot penetrate it. Perhaps through devotion to life and an attempt to make friends with the depth of our inner darkness we can free our imagination to search for, and our ego to accept, the paradoxically small and crucially important part we play in whatever process life is.

If we accept the analogy of alchemy that life is a process of transformation, we can see that we are a part of the metamorphosis of creation, reflected in our inner self and in our outer self, where the imperishable is being removed from the perishable, the true from the false, so that both may move on and grow into the future.[4] We cannot abandon our hard-won rational position and return to nature, even though in many ways it is our foundation. We must be aware of our foundation in nature and search further to enrich our consciousness. Our true humanity is evoked—if we can stand it. As our awareness of death grows, it is a time to suffer and a time to treasure, a time to become more fully alive.

Life is the great adventure. Most of the great literary epics have chronicled this adventure, this journey. Life demands to be lived, is worth living, and in the words of Laurens Van Der Post,[5] "... is always worth living and one fights life for life's sake until life decides, through its own experiences, that the time has come to bring the fight to an end."

This is the Western way, our way. We are the vessels in which the transformational work takes place. Life's experiences are the heat that provides the energy for the work. The face of our own death and the acceptance of our own conflicts and suffering allow us to grasp the notion of suffering through participation, through *compassion*—a notion with which our current society has a great deal of trouble staying in touch, leading us unconsciously to flood our world with violence and pain.

But our way is, by its very nature, a struggle. We are the vessel where the inner world, the outer world, and the eternal world meet and are interwoven, and we may find that our outer conflicts reflect our lack of an inner ability to grow into the truth of ourselves. The symbolic meaning of "The Way of the Cross" stands devastatingly before a culture that idolizes material prosperity and social recognition as rewards for living, for conventional rectitude. The Eastern approach, the emptying of desire in the personality, is not for us. Westerners who seek this way are usually looking for an easy way out and fail to consider the vigor, the discipline, and the ferocious battle for life in Eastern cultures, not to mention the immense difference between their view and our view of the

---

4   Laurens Van Der Post, *About Blady: A Pattern Out of Time* (New York: William Morrow, 1991), 22.

5   Van Der Post, *About Blady*, 15.

sanctity of the individual human life. Many Westerners trying to follow these paths end up wanderers in the misty land of illusion, outside the streams of life. Perhaps someday these two ways will come together, but it isn't likely to happen today.

The ancient Greeks thought of another kind of peace, an additional meaning for *eirene*. Plato later considered it the "profound peace" of the old, when they no longer need to be concerned about passion. Maybe, just maybe, we have interpreted this idea too casually. Perhaps, in reality, this is peace that results from a maturity of perspective, an appreciation of the gift of life with all of its ambivalent heat.

Chapter 7

AFTERNOON REFLECTIONS

In the Belly of Life

In his book *Fire In The Belly: On Being a Man*, Sam Keen,[1] one of my favorite authors, presents a premise that I stumbled over. He suggests that as men embark into life, two questions are important: "Where am I going?" and "Who is going with me?"—the "who" in this instance referring to a woman. Keen then points out that if a man gets these questions out of the above order, he is in trouble. Reading his statements gave me a mind jolt, requiring that I stop and ponder them.

Since early adolescence I have been one of those men who seems to have had these questions out of order. And generally I have been "in trouble." But I must say that this turmoil has often guided my growth and determined my destiny. I do not even think my inner teacher is particularly interested in my having a linear or trouble-free life. As a society, we often seem to think there is an order for things that works well—if we can only find it. However, if I were to follow this line of thought, I would find myself confronted by one of Jung's strongest statements: "Anyone who takes the sure road is as good as dead."[2]

I continued my musing by wondering if Keen's assumptions

---

1   Sam Keen, *Fire In The Belly: On Being a Man* (New York: Bantam, 1991), 12.
2   C.G. Jung, *Memories, Dreams, Reflections*, ed. A. Jaffé, trans. Richard and Clara Winston (New York: Pantheon, 1973), 297.

might reflect an attitude toward life that is a little too cerebral or might imply there is a way for "getting it right." In other words, a way to be in control and minimize or avoid "trouble," conflict, and suffering. Might this position ignore the notions of fate and destiny, the importance of confrontation and encounter, and the value of losing and then finding ourselves in our search for an inner compass? Can such a perspective overvalue the rational mind and perhaps reflect an assumption that we have no inner teacher at all?

What if we imagine that *each* woman a man encounters marks his destiny? Along these lines, Jung answered a letter to a man having a series of problematic marriages by saying, "In practice it means that the woman of your choice represents your own task you did not understand."[3] Perhaps each encounter could bring to a man an experience of himself and fetch parts of himself into his life so he could assimilate them into his consciousness—though the process might take many years and she might have left his life long before the consciousness she stimulated was realized. Would this self-realization be worth the trouble? Suppose Odysseus had stayed home trying to solve these problems and avoided the "Odyssey"? Would he ever have been able to truly find home, as in the lines of T.S. Eliot in "Little Gidding"?

> *We shall not cease from exploration*
> *And the end of all our exploring*
> *Will be to arrive where we started*
> *And know the place for the first time.*

As I recall the "Odyssey," almost every turning point in the story was marked by a feminine figure with whom Odysseus had made no conscious decision to become involved or even to meet. What if Christ had remained in his carpenter shop, possibly lying on the couch of his rabbi twice a week, trying to solve the dilemmas

---

3   C.G. Jung, *C.G. Jung Letters* 2, ed. G. Adler in collaboration with A. Jaffé, trans. R.F.C. Hull London (Routledge & Kegan Paul, 1976), 320.

of life as though they were abstract or rational problems? Where can this logical attitude leave us in relationship to developing and understanding the story of our life?

We must have living experience, especially of trouble and conflict, or we have nothing real to reflect upon or to gain insight into. And if we continue our pursuit of consciousness, we must continually put our self-knowledge into practice and begin the search for consciousness anew. Otherwise we are simply playing mind games. Keen is correct in one sense, however. Putting the great twosome, male and female, together and going somewhere in life is no small endeavor, and I believe we will experience plenty of trouble in this area as we live, no matter how we attempt to order Keen's questions.

In our psyche, we also have two consummate *others* to deal with: the conscious and the unconscious. To this Jung added two additional, elemental "others," which I mentioned earlier. He called the feminine in the man the *anima* and the masculine in the woman the *animus*. (He borrowed these two terms from the almost forgotten language of the early Christian era, when the world was more vividly inflamed by power and love.)

These elemental figures—the anima and the animus—connect our conscious and unconscious selves repeatedly throughout our lives. Our experience of this connection brings healing and wholeness, then plunges us back into the stream of life again. If we consciously relate to the anima and the animus, we can substantially enrich our lives.

We meet them most often as projections onto living "others." As our lives progress so do these encounters and confrontations, on many different levels. Conceivably, differentiating the projected image and its essence from its outer carriers may be a major part of a life's journey. At times, these outer carriers may also act as healing islands in our lives, or turning points, as they did for Odysseus. At other times, they may guide us, as Beatrice initiated Dante's journey, opening both inner and outer vistas.

Trying to be too intellectual about these matters leads to an attempt to reduce them to concepts. Then we have a tendency to take life externally, at mere face value, and risk losing our greatest opportunities for encountering our deeper instincts and transformational patterns. In such instances, we lose the parts of ourselves that can carry us toward the destiny, the personal pattern, we were born to fulfill. We risk missing our own lives. On the other hand, we must also resist the temptation to live impulsively, for such a simplistic, unconscious approach to life would cause us to lose the entire meaning of consciousness.

I believe we should note that transformational encounters do not depend as much on gender as they do on psychological structure, and in one form or another they are timeless components of the human story. Suppose one is a woman or is gay. Can we not surmise that the patterns will be the same as they would be for anyone else, that the encounters will be just as meaningful, and that life will require just as much courage?

The Elemental Other

The organized professional or institutional mind of our (or perhaps any) time, stranded in a remote desert of abstractions between art and science and focused on efficiency, yearns, even if unconsciously, for the courage to encounter ancient mysteries. When people who are caught in their professional personas enter the somewhat obscure atmosphere in which I work, they often feel a little out of kilter. Without their realizing it, their professional identity may slip quietly out of the room as eros enters, dislocating their persona, as in the following story.

Following his customary pattern, an analysand bustled into my office, greeted me, and sat down. Opening his briefcase, he briskly handed me copies of his notes, dreams, and journal entries for the past week. He was a professional man, prepared to ensure that his time was well spent.

I sat forward in my chair, listening. Focused, attentive, I can appear professional, too. He began by saying, "I had a strange dream last night. I was at a church retreat, attending seminars with my wife. I looked over her shoulder. She had her seminar book open. Inside of it she was looking at a graphic selection of what we used to call 'French postcards.' That's all I remember."

I paused for a minute before responding, remembering that sexuality usually seems particularly difficult for competent, successful-appearing men to discuss. Slowly I responded, "What comes to mind from these images?"

His manner changed. He sat forward, talking quietly and thoughtfully. "I was thinking about this dream on the way over here. My wife used to have a fantasy. I guess she had it for several years and then she quit having it, or quit telling me about it."

"Yes," I said.

"She thought we should go to the Peabody Hotel in Memphis. You know, the fancy one with the ducks swimming around in a pool in the lobby."

I nodded.

"We both would dress elegantly. She would go into the lounge, sit at the bar, and order a cocktail. I'd walk in like a stranger, see her, and be immediately attracted. Then I would come over and strike up a conversation."

By this time his voice was hushed; he continued sitting forward, looking at me intently. I paused, waiting for that feminine voice in my head to help me out. What an opportunity for her to give a lecture on how "we" men take sexuality too simply, how we need to learn a few things about romance, creativity, attention, tenderness, appreciation, and intimacy. I sat quietly. Silence.

Far back in myself I heard another voice, male, maybe fourteen or fifteen, saying, "My God, that would scare me to death." I sat back, ran those words through my professional persona, and repeated them aloud.

The memories of those delicate, vulnerable years when eros is beginning to lurk just around an interior corner in all of us. Even after a good marriage, with children grown or well on their way, eros will call us again to face its classic ordeal—to have courage and maybe, just maybe, open ourselves anew and thereby gain a little more personal authenticity. And, wherever eros is, a spiritual task will not be far behind. For whether it is regressive or progressive, eros requires us to face a personal choice of some kind, usually ethical or moral, at each encounter.

Once the common gold is won, we must learn to come into relationship with life once again. If we look backward to the age of mythology, our elemental reference chart, we find that Odysseus is required to stop in the middle of his journey and visit the underworld. There he must talk with his mother and seek direction from the blind seer, Tiresias. The seer informs him that after his quest is completed and his kingdom is restored, he will have to make a sacrifice to each of the gods and goddesses.

Two things become apparent when we reflect upon this episode. Before his quest can be completed, he has to return to his inner nature, dialogue with his origins, and ask for guidance. Then, when his journey is completed and his tasks are achieved, he will have to return to each of the primary sources of animating energy in his nature, with humility and respect, in order to have a more complete relationship with them. This procedure is charted in his nature and is charted in the nature of every one of us. We must return to our yearnings, wounds, and vulnerabilities so they may carry us deeper into our unfulfilled task of becoming truly and totally human.

Adolescence is a time of yearning—a yearning for the future and a yearning for unity with another. It is also a time of yearning to be out of childhood. Many of us, however, enter this period wounded, unprepared, and without the strength for such a passage. We may marry to fulfill this anguished yearning, often thinking we are on top of things. Such a marriage has a tendency to become a "mythological ordeal," as our inner teacher tries to initiate us into adulthood.

A lesson plan for this passage is available to our inner teacher in the myth of Eros and Psyche, as Eros was separated from his mother, Aphrodite, and went through many trials and ordeals in order to achieve masculine maturing. Likewise, Psyche traveled her own arduous path to separate from her family and her illusions to attain feminine maturing. As the tale ends, they seem prepared to live happily thereafter.

The same may not be true for us, though. For us, the interior psychological meaning of completing this lesson plan may be greater than the outer experience of an actual relationship. Once we have finished this particular lesson from our inner teacher, our outer life may not be to our liking—we may face a bitter or sorrowful divorce or the need to sacrifice a cherished fantasy, ideal, or illusion. Our inner teacher doesn't take life's lesson plans from the curricula of our parents, church, society, or Walt Disney. They come instead from the archetypal patterns that seek to guide us into individuation.

Sex is always difficult. It contains the pain and ecstasy that continually initiate us into life, whether we are willing or not. Sex brings more people into crisis and dissatisfaction with their lives and therefore into analysis, psychotherapy, and counseling than any other issue. It can lead us repeatedly to a confrontation with our inner nature and to subterranean feelings that remind us, decade after decade, that they have a mind of their own, no matter how strong our defensive fortress may have become. Sex has a power that is numinous and ominous, powerful, awe-inspiring, and dangerous—a fact that the primitive recognized and we seem to have forgotten. They treated it with reverence; and while we may idolize it, we have little reverence for it. As a result, it tortures us, personally and collectively, and will continue to do so until, individually, we learn to revere our own nature.

Sex education, techniques, and the popular self-help literature offer little relief in this area. Medicine, psychology, and education have followed the lead of religious institutions by taking our behaviors at face value, stripping them of their subjective connections, and, in their own way, labeling them in a pejorative manner as "functional" or "dysfunctional." But by the afternoon of life we should have learned to be very careful how we label issues of eros that are at the timeless heart of life, especially the so-called "dys-functional" acts of love. A so-called misdeed may reflect an inner necessity and a rigid correctiveness may smother the spirit of life. For example, the misdeeds of Romeo and Juliet led them, through love, to a tragedy that stopped a feud and reunited a city divided against itself. An infidelity, properly understood, may transform a life or even a marriage. Sexual transgressions may be required for an adolescent to differentiate from an overbearing family. Or, sexual transgressions may be needed to threaten an overly rigid society into opening itself.

"Fidelity" and "infidelity" are examples of labels that, when taken too simply and unequivocally, can destroy a life. A more judicious perspective harnesses us to a search for deeper meaning in what we do and makes our decisions more profound, though not easier. It turns our impulses into moral choices based on a willingness to suffer and impose suffering on others. Along these lines, Jungian analyst Irene de Castillejo[4] offers us a boundary-crossing paradox for our consideration. She suggests that spouses who protect their mate from the knowledge of infidelity may also be protecting their mate from the pain necessary for individuation.

Creativity, sexuality, and spirituality are essential instincts in our nature. Sexuality and spirituality supply the impetus toward the creativity that, in the art of living and the creation of culture, is expressed as well as symbolized by the archetypal image of the *child*.

Eros is the greatest tool of the inner teacher, who uses it repeatedly to connect us to our place in the web of life. Time and again, eros leads us into our illusions and life pushes us out again. We might imagine that the funeral of our illusions is where we glean another small measure of life's reality. We may also conjecture that the "hardheaded realist," the cynic with "no illusions," is living in the greatest denial humanly possible. If we can stand the stress of inner funerals, our youthful feelings will return to us for further

---

4   Irene C. de Castillejo, *Knowing Woman* (New York: Putnam, 1973), 124.

differentiation and may eventually lead us to a capacity for love that expresses an increasing sense of wholeness, eternally symbolized in the royal marriage of the masculine and feminine principles.

Intrinsic Essence

Like all initially unconscious material, our masculine and feminine characteristics can only come into consciousness through projections. Initially, as projections, they are external and out of our conscious awareness. As a result of our developing awareness, they are slowly recognized, taken back as our own, and reformulated into our personality. Eros, following its inherent creative patterns over time, is often our connecting energy to these figures. In our lives, it more or less follows an elemental blueprint, one that is adapted to our particular situation by our hidden teacher.

In a general conceptualization of life's progress, we might suppose that our first awareness of being buffeted by eros appears when we initially fall in love. On this particular track, we may end up marrying one of the "others." As life moves on and we approach noontime, we may find the romance has worn thin. In psychological terms, this would mean the projections have worn thin. Then we could either look for a new "other" to project onto, hoping thereby to stir our atrophy, or we could choose a second alternative. We could begin the difficult process of reclaiming our projected contents and love our partner in a deeper, more personal way. That would involve loving our partner for his or her human self, the part he or she has played in our shared lives, and being *loving* rather than *in love*. This pattern, of which I have presented only as an over-simplified version, seems to be considered the normal course by many psychologists for the beginning and maturing of love in relationships. Jung and numerous others have written about these issues and, while they are important, the directions I wish to explore are different. I want to stay more closely attuned to the turning points and the healings with which eros presents us and the desire that weaves our being, inner and outer, into the web of life.

Let us begin by envisioning a young professional woman. Her life has been a long migration from the tangled thicket of childhood. Her father had been one of those in-between men in the military—a warrant officer. Neither a member of the officer corps nor the enlisted ranks, he was a specialist in machines. He was seldom home. When he was home, he was generally drunk or headed in that direction.

One of her earliest memories was of following him around while he worked on the pile of cars in their yard. She was just beyond the toddling stage, her father's helper, fetching the tools he wanted. His communications to her were guttural, and often cursed when she made the mistake of presenting the wrong tool with her tiny hands.

He never treasured her the way a child should be treasured, nor did he respond to her simple, childlike adoration. She did not give up, however, and faithfully helped him for years. From this early world of her father, men, and machines, she retained a feeling of poignant insignificance; a haunting question had been structured into her psyche like a broken record, *"What about me?"*

Such early questions shade all of our relationships until we resolve them. Our experiences with our parents are the first we have of eros and they imprint their patterns in us as we are formed. These models last a long time, and coming to grips with them requires that substantial energy be directed toward developing conscious awareness. They pattern our relationships with ourselves as well as with others. One can imagine how these early emotional experiences affected her inner development, that they were like placing a stone atop a seedling as it began to grow.

Early in adolescence, as her identity was struggling to develop and find its way around this stone, she met the young man she would later marry. Seeking nourishment and security, she became deeply involved with him and adopted herself into his family. He was the quiet, calm son of a stable, warm, though somewhat remote couple. Sex quickly sealed his attraction to her. They were married in their late teens and helped each other through college, graduate school, and into professions. She had become a Certified Public Accountant in a position that gave her a lot of freedom and money and the ability to move around.

As the morning of her life was running into the afternoon, she found herself in an affair she could not get out of, and this predicament brought her to my office. The affair seemed to have run its course. She could see the man for who he was—fairly good-looking, not too bright, and with little regard for women. He was married, had children, and, she had discovered, was involved with several women besides herself. Unfortunately, even this knowledge did not help her give him up. In his own way, he was a master at the art of ambiguity and of keeping women hooked in a hopeless pursuit of what seemed to be a potential relationship. In a certain way, she even saw him as pitiful and wanted to help him mature or develop the capacity to appreciate life and love. (Over the decades, she had grown to see her father as pitiful as well, but beyond her help.)

Meanwhile, knowing about her affair, her husband maintained his position as a good, stable man. He remained patient, waiting while she went through what he considered a *stage*. As one might guess, he had now become a hard-working, successful executive who was seldom home and had missed over a decade of her camouflaged pleas for attention: "What about me?" True to his heritage (the heritage that was initially so attractive and important to her), nothing ever rattled him, not even his wife's needs or her affairs.

One afternoon I was sitting in my office watching the rain and musing about what kind of man (actually men, for I have heard this story more than once) thinks his wife is going through a *stage* when she has an affair, especially when this *stage* seems to continue year after year. While relaxed and ruminating, I heard that feminine voice from deep in my own psyche telling me, "Men are so emotionally retarded. They turn their wives into witches and bitches with their blind behavior and single-minded, pigheaded approach to life."

"What approach?" I silently asked.

"The one they call rational or sensible!" she retorted. "This poor woman has been trying for years to make her husband realize there are more valuable things in life than what their narrow approach includes and he thinks she's going through a *stage* for God's sake! He doesn't even have the sense to get mad."

"You're right about that," I replied. "I don't understand it myself. But why don't women simply say what they want?"

She replied, "First of all, we don't want you to simply be some kind of compliant, co-dependent android, just trying to keep us happy and placated. We want to be treasured and respected and treated in a way that *shows* it. Furthermore, we don't want to have to be happy all the time just so you can stay in a good mood. We want to be interacted with in whatever reality we are experiencing."

"I know," I thought to myself. I knew that many women want to be able to argue with a man without the argument being oriented toward violence or winning and losing. They want men to show caring and be directed toward grinding out personal and relational clarity and appreciation. Such a process can also be extremely helpful to men if they can ever learn it.

She continued. "On the other hand, we're scared. People quit so easily these days. It's hard as hell to love yourself, or anybody, when abandonment seems to always be lurking around the corner. These are scary times for love and values. Women have learned well enough that 'The best man for the job is a woman!' Love and romance past the physical level has become pretty terrifying. Everybody's scared."

"Hmm," I replied.

"Don't forget I'm a part of you," she finished.

"Scary," I thought.

As the young woman in my story continued her analytic work, she had the following dream:

> I was alone in my house late at night. I received a phone
> call telling me there was a prowler in the neighborhood,
> a very dangerous man. I felt safe. I knew the doors and

windows were locked. Then I realized I had left the back door unlocked. I rushed down the stairs and was standing in the living room. Almost at once I realized I was naked from the waist down and he was already in the house.

This dream marked a turning point in her experience and set the stage for her to be able to face her fear of masculine power and the vulnerability she felt due to not having been valued by her father. The image of the intruder in women's dreams often heralds the beginning of a transformation process in their personality that is healing a wound left by their father. The intruder represents primitive masculine energy that needs to be recognized and refined until it supports her authenticity with personal power.

Once this transformation began, she was no longer bound to seeking affirmation from men in her outer life. Her analytic work proceeded and her outer problem was resolved as it transformed into an inner conflict, closer to the habitat of the deeper issue. She was led in this direction by eros, her attraction to men, and by her ability to grasp the lesson offered by her inner teacher. Of course, this turning point was not an end. It was a beginning, and as she continues changing who she is, changing how she is living must follow.

In this example, we can trace the outline that the inner lesson plan was following and the intertwining of eros, growth, and healing. Starting in the outer world of childhood, the masculine essence (or animus) within this woman was imprinted by her father. (A woman's emotional experience of her father is the foundation for the development of her animus and her "masculine" attitudes toward herself.) The wounds she suffered in their encounters sought healing as she entered adolescence and life wished to continue more creatively.

Once she had solidified her identity and began her healing (through her husband and his family), the momentum carried her into adulthood. Then, as her adult life consolidated, a longing for new vitality and further healing erupted again as an outer attraction to a lover. This attraction could not be given up without a psychological regression—until there was both an inner and an outer shift, a transformation in her psyche along the lines I have outlined.

In this situation, we might surmise that she was doubly fortunate. She already had an inner directedness and the ability to work in analysis, and she and her husband valued each other enough to hold the tension of their relationship and work on it. Thus, as the tension eased in her struggle with the outer men in her life due to her devoted attention to healing, the doorway to her inner work opened with the intruder dream. With this interior event, her analysis became more clearly focused as a process of growth and enrichment, as *individuation*.

An inner healing had taken place and a new kind of masculine energy had penetrated her psychic space. When she cultivates it and relates to it, this new masculine energy will become part of her personality. It will bring in a new sense of the sensual, the physical, and the powerful to support her being "one within herself," and as she transforms, her relationships—personal and otherwise—will have to change as well. As "steadfast" as her husband has been, he will have to open to a new level of growth and intimacy or face increasing tensions in the marriage again, even though her growth has led her to a deeper understanding of his place in her life and an enhanced appreciation of him as a person.

Such lessons are not just for people in the first half of life. Growth can follow the eros path as long as we are open to it. I know one seventy-five-year-old gentleman who has spent the last three years resolving, in a series of sculptures, a teenage love affair that ended badly. In his outer life it resolved long ago and he subsequently had a long and vital marriage. But underneath, he had experienced a layer of melancholy that was now coming to its completion, expressed in stone, after six decades.

My reflections along these lines brought to mind a recent experience I had with another man, an analysand who is a few years older than I, in the late afternoon of life. He is also a therapist.

We were nearing the end of the analytic hour. Sitting across from me, aware that he would be turning sixty years old in a few days, he was looking beyond my shoulder and through the window behind me. He gazed beyond the city rooftops, between two church steeples, and toward the mountains in the far background. As he talked, his eyes did not return to the room until he was ready to leave. He was saying, "I thought about her on and off almost all week. I had only a brief glimpse of her last week in a dream. It's been months since I thought of her. It's been over twenty years since we met, shortly after my first wife and I separated. God! What a nightmare that time was.

"We never even made love, you know. We spent our last day together lying side by side, nude. She was married and I was crazy. I have finished this obsession! I had lunch with her two years ago and there was nothing.

"All week I have wanted to call her," he continued. "I've picked up the phone a dozen times between sessions. It wouldn't work. It's only a *projection*. I've worked this through! I've finished it!"

"Oh, crap," I thought. People who talk about love as just a projection miss the point. Therapists are often the worst in this regard. Too many want to skip life and get right to the concepts, almost as if they think they can begin at the end. It doesn't work. There is no growth and no future in this approach. Life requires a commitment to participation. It is not an abstract experience.

"Have you really finished it?" I queried. "It sounds as if some kind of longing is still there, is here right now."

"No, I've finished with that!"

I pushed a little. "It doesn't sound like 'that' has finished with you. Perhaps there's some kind of thread here. Can we look for it?"

"Should I call her?" he asked.

"Calling her wouldn't mean you have to run away with her. How do you imagine you would feel? What was it like before?"

"I felt alive, crazy, screwed up—alive! Our time is up. I've got a meeting. I have to go."

THE JOURNEY INTO WHOLENESS

Thankful for the clock, he hurried out. Obviously, he stated a truth in those final few words and was relieved that his busy, professional schedule saved him from having to face it.

The image of a woman within a man, his anima, functions in a manner similar to that of the evolving masculine image we traced in the story of the young woman. These images begin with a parental imprint from a man's mother. Present or absent, parents make an imprint that, to a greater or lesser extent, matches the elemental blueprint in his psychic structure. The degree of matching or mismatching affects his psychological development and how he may have to work with it in the future. A sister or a brother will often provide a modifying influence on this imprint and help the developing inner image of the feminine move from under the parental ambiance until it is projected upon a "beloved" outside of the home. Sibling experience also helps him be a little more grounded in his projections, as his experiences with siblings may remind him that the anonymous "other" to whom he is attracted may have a very human side he is failing to see.

If a man's early wound is sufficiently serious, he may be too afraid to be open to a "beloved" and become attached to someone from an emotionally compensatory standpoint. For example, a man with a cold, demanding mother may seek a lover or a wife who will nurture him warmly and unconditionally. In one form or another, a man's anima is generally projected outward in adolescence and begins weaving its developmental path through his life. If he becomes aware of it and consciously relates to it, then it becomes the bridge that connects him to his depths. It also compensates his social personality or identity, his persona, always trying to bring balance and vitality to it.

I believe that the therapist in the above story had become too comfortable and isolated in his social and professional identity. His inner teacher may have presented the image of this woman—in psychological terms, an upsetting anima figure—in an effort to urge his unfaithfulness to the smothering security of his self-imposed conventions. Her image creates a longing for devotion, love, romance, risk, bitchiness, and vitality.

In general, the beloved promises this vitality. The appearance or especially the reappearance of an older image symbolizes a need. It brings up a yearning for vitality and a desire for a creative future. It leads us to be attentive to the patterns arising within us and to the knowledge that we must lovingly make these things foremost in our life. The appearance of these images awakens us, calling to mind our need to return repeatedly to the wellspring of our nature, the unconscious, to revitalize ourselves. If we don't, we will become possessed by these aspects of ourselves or by the depression that ensues, because we are throttling them.

Our recognizing these animus and anima figures is crucial in the afternoon of life, for this is the time when we can learn not to worship them externally and not to succumb to them internally. We can develop a conscious appreciation of them and, thereby, a relationship with them. Then a depression or an attraction may transform from unconscious longing into inner becoming. These images come from an inner mentor who wants to call up a more vibrant future for us, wants new things to emerge within and without in our lives, and wants to observe the inner laws of our being rather than the dull pathways in which we so easily seek contentment.

Later, after finishing my last hour of work, I sat back to reflect for a few minutes, to bring closure to my day. My mind began veering away from its working focus. I recalled that earlier session. "Sweet," I thought. "Two middle-aged children, lost in the woods of life, lying nude, side by side, throughout a day, comforting each other."

"Sentimental mush," my inner She replied, intruding into my reverie. "Women are meant to be made love to, not spiritualized in some syrupy, sentimental manner and then abandoned because you don't have the guts to touch them."

"Men *need* to spiritualize women occasionally," I answered. "If we didn't, if Dante hadn't spiritualized Beatrice, we wouldn't have the *Divine Comedy* and countless other works of art."

"I didn't see any Dantes in your office today. Go watch *Zorba* again," she scoffed.

"I'm trying to unwind," I answered. "Go back to your cave, cathedral, or whatever, and leave me alone."

As she left I heard a definite, "Pff't, pff't."

The sound reminded me of Irene Pappas, the wonderful Greek actress who so powerfully portrayed the widow in the movie version of Nikos Kazantzakis' book *Zorba the Greek*. That sound carried the venomous Mediterranean intensity she expressed as she spat at the men who were badgering her in the village tavern. It was a simple expressive act that conveyed more angry contempt than a feminist march on Washington. "Damn!" I thought, "An anima figure like Irene Pappas could stop a man in his tracks."

Much of Kazantzakis' work haunts me when I am in a reflective mood. At such times I am frequently visited by the specter of the widow's violent fate. Clearly, she personified the image of Aphrodite, the goddess of love, life, fertility, and renewal, who exemplifies the individuating eros that impacts us personally and weaves us into the web of life. Long before the arrival of the Greek pantheon, she had been a mother goddess, spinning the skein of life.

The movie easily replays in my mind. I see that intense, independent, beautiful woman brutally murdered before and by the townspeople. She was murdered for refusing to live either the romantic or the sexual fantasies of the men in that tavern, while at the same time remaining a living symbol of emotional threat to the women. The old women began stoning her, yelping, "Kill her! Kill her!" for they had turned murderous in the bitter trap of convention rather than wise with their years.

The murder took place in the churchyard. The priests conducting a funeral mass never paused to try to save her. They proceeded, deaf and blind to the agony of life. The funeral itself was for a boy too young and too weak to embrace her, a boy who, in a helpless state of love and despair, had drowned himself in the sea. "Boss," the contemplative man, the man of books and insight, had neither the presence nor the physical authority to help her. He sent a poor, young, half-witted man to fetch Zorba, the grizzled man of action. Even Zorba, though strong, was alone and had not sufficient resources to rescue her. Her throat was cut by the constable, the man whose duty it was to enforce collective authority.

Zorba and Boss represent two modes of masculinity that are deep in conflict in our time. (Though even many women, in trying to be *fair* or to see both sides of the issue, murder their basic feminine values, the values that could help them change their lives—or more accurately, truly live their lives. These women become lost in a sea of indecision, cut off from their feeling function, the gateway of eros. This stance can only lead, at some point, to a militant, angry, despairing response toward life.)

Kazantzakis portrayed a fundamental scene in our time. The feminine, the carrier of the image of individuating eros, lies murdered, bleeding to death on the earth in the face of a fragmented, impotent masculinity. Symbolically, this story is repeating itself in the soul of each of us, regardless of our gender. Daily I encounter both men and women who are unwittingly murdering their feminine soul for the sake of practicality, convention, identity, achievement, and equality, presenting a paradox of sadness in the time of feminism.

Realizing now that darkness had come, I felt tired, ready to go home for the evening. I remembered that She is never far away and that we have yet to understand what her presence fully means or how we are going to grow beyond the past we have created today.

Moments of Truth

A river of folk stores, literature, art, and music spanning many centuries now flows from our past. The theme of eros, fate, and their intertwining to shape human destiny is constant over the millennia. Even so, in this age of literalism and institutionalized personalities, we try to live in a cloud of denial, one that robs our lives of the meanings of the heart, the ageless symbol of vitality and courage.

The river of creative expression tells us that the turning points in our personal dramas are the products of great moments of eros.

A recent event in my life reminded me of how sorely we miss the truth of these experiences. A friend telephoned me, wanting to meet for lunch at a pleasant sidewalk café. He is a large Hemingwayish type of man, well into middle age, whose handlebar mustache adds a touch of elegance to his countenance. But in contrast to that size and appearance, he has a somewhat quizzical ambiance, looking as though he is a bit confused at being on this planet. He wanted to chat with me about a mutual friend who was currently living with him.

My Hemingwayish friend began his adult life as an architect and had gone on to mix this profession with city planning. Around the noontime of his life, he decided painting was a stronger call and gradually moved in that direction. Blocked as a painter, he moved into sculpture, his present vocation, in which he was blocked again.

Early in his adulthood, he moved to a small Caribbean island country and proceeded to guzzle his way through several marriages. For a while he was socially close to government officials, and those relationships resulted in commissions for a number of official building projects. During this same period, in a fit of pique over some small issue, he renounced his American citizenship. This act was purely personal and had nothing whatsoever to do with the greater issues confronting Americans in the troubled '60s and '70s. Shortly thereafter, as regimes in that area of the world are prone to do, the government in this small country changed. The new government threw him out because of his former affiliations and he returned to the U.S. Nowadays our circle of friends gets a kick out of the fact that he is the only person we know who is officially an alien in his own hometown.

In contrast, our mutual friend had followed a more traditional pattern of life that included marriage, a family, and being a partner in a large advertising agency, where he worked for over two decades. Beginning in their creative department, he got himself on an illustrious professional track that carried him into the position of a managing partner. Before he quite realized what was happening, he was north-side-of-town affluent. The benefits of his new status included a country club membership, private schools for his children, management responsibilities—and being bored silly. After feeling stuck for a few years, he fell in love with a woman who was new to town and worked at a competing agency. Some of our friends thought she was sexy and flirtatious in a dangerous sort of way, cool and devouring. Others felt she was a lovely person—gentle, creative, and warm. Regardless, she clearly had a mind of her own.

Our friend left his family and his firm and, fired with creative energy, began pursuing his long-time dream of writing a novel. Then one day, out of the blue, his girlfriend abandoned him. In fact, she left town with the former partner in a large accounting firm. Our friend was devastated.

He was now living in a small, one-room studio in our sculptor friend's backyard. The sculptor told me the man was out there day after day. He reported, "He's filled up every damn thing in the place with cigarette butts. Ashtrays, cups, saucers, glasses, bowls, plates, bottles. He smokes and drinks Scotch, then goes out for more and starts over again.

"Is he still writing?" I inquired.

"Yes, more than ever."

"Are you worried?" I continued. "Do you think we should do something?"

"Hell, yes, I'm worried," he replied. "But not about him."

"Then what?" I exclaimed.

His eyes, bruised with emotion, lifted slowly until they were level with mine. "You're the analyst," he said, with a grimness that matched my surprise. "I'm worried about me. I wish I could love like that."

The look in my friend's eyes reminded me of Jung's poignant statement in *Modern Man in Search of a Soul*: "Who are forgiven their many sins? Those who have loved much. But to those who have loved little, their few sins are held against them." Love opens us to life in a way nothing else can. Once we lock it away or lose it, no matter how good the reason and no matter how otherwise interesting and successful we appear, we deeply fear we may never find the key again. And if we are not careful, that's exactly what may happen. Neither Freud nor Jung thought we should barricade ourselves against or isolate ourselves from the transformational power of our instincts. In response to our fear, Jung noted, "Love, we find out, is the power of fate."

Frequently there is a story within a story, and you may have spotted a second theme in my account. Let us visualize the events I have related as though they are a mythic tale and look for an underlying theme. If we move from a literal to a symbolic viewpoint, the woman can be regarded as representing life. In this case, one man embraces her, first feeling ecstasy and then despair. Another man observes and wishes he too could participate in such an embrace.

Of course, this story should not be literalized as a concrete guide to living. But it *is* meant as a symbolic comment to help us understand our nature and particularly the courage that is required to accept despair as part of the price for ecstasy, and often as part of the price that must be paid for personal creativity and authenticity.

Eros, in its way, is always trying to bring us home to ourselves. The masculine principle as a mythic element represents creative achievement, the bringing of potentials into actuality. When the masculine energy is not serving life, eros attempts to break the conventional focus, perhaps with a Circe or temptress figure, as in my story.

Symbolically, the woman represented vitality that once glimpsed, seduced the man into a process that fractured the conventional mold he had trapped himself in and freed his creativity. Such a fracture caused pain and suffering because it fragmented the self-image he had worked hard to build. This pain usually follows the ecstasy of the moment of breaking free. And such a process hurt others as well, because he was no longer the person they imagined him to be—he was no longer reliable in their eyes. By contrast, my Hemingwayish friend *appeared* to be a man who had lived an unusual and even creative life. But he realized that he had never loved life deeply enough to break free of his self-image and risk despair.

We have "fields," professions, careers, and endless social expectations placed on us. We may try to "rise above" our erotic self or to deny it, but following either of these directions carries us away from ourselves, just as the requirements of our professional life and social position sometimes do. Eros is a tool for returning us to the state of being human, to our homeland. Individuating eros generates a language and a striving that ultimately penetrates the surface of our life. Do we yearn for sex, union, wholeness, growth, success, or perhaps just for life? In any event, when we are seized by eros, we must allow it to move us, as it asks us to burst our boundaries. As that happens, we find that we are searching for a way—often dreamed of and fantasized about, but in reality, not yet known—to transcend ourselves.

As we saw in the previous story, eros cannot be evaluated or measured in conventional terms. And it is not simply "getting what you want." It requires that we embrace life and then allow our relationship to ripen, trusting that the barrenness of winter will be followed by the flowering of spring. The passion and pain of love torture and purify us as they burn away our one-sided allegiance to whatever leads us away from the human heart and personal authenticity. Sometimes eros traps us in a boiling inner cauldron. We may wish to flee from the person to whom we are tied because of the dependence and sacrifice involved in our staying. Eros forces us to become conscious of the path we have laid out unconsciously as part of our destiny. It leads us to risk everything and, in this process, leads us back to ourselves. In bygone times, love and drunkenness were considered great healing processes for the soul and body. Eros, the god of love, was also known as the "purifier of the soul," and Dionysus, the god of wine, held the key that fragmented the forms that enmesh us.

The sorrows of love and loss penetrate to our center if we can stand it. Self-awareness helps us heal in a way that produces inner strength, a widening in consciousness, and a discovery of emotions and deeper meaning within ourselves.

In primitive times, masculine initiation ceremonies taught courage and the endurance of pain, while feminine ceremonies taught patience and waiting, focusing on the cycles of nature as well as on a resistance to sentimental pity. Perhaps the time has come for all of us to be initiated in both of these forms. Maybe eros is leading us into this agenda. If such is the case, relationships may lead to increased self-consciousness rather than demanding its suffocation, as our past social and religious structures seemed to advocate. We may find ourselves less likely to fall prey to destructive relationships within and without. And even though relationships have much to teach us, every lesson does not have to be bitter. Many people seem to make the mistake of choosing the bitter path as a defense rather than as a way to learn. They end up "falling in love" with their jaundiced attitudes and life-avoiding self-pity, which frequently shows up in frightful dreams, reflecting the collective images prevalent in horror movies—murderous, violent, and often seductive and sexual.

Summing Up—Connecting to the Center

Anima and animus are psychological terms. They represent our efforts to get a handle on the elemental principles beneath the inner characteristics that are fundamentally opposite to our conscious experience of ourselves. They represent, in general terms, feminine and masculine principles that are far too comprehensive to be contained in a single person and too complex to define a gender in a literal sense. Once we have opened our inner eye in their direction, they may seem hopelessly complex, but familiarity with them can ease that confusion and increase our sense of wonder about our own nature.

They are among the elemental strata in our nature that are part of the collective unconscious, which represent and sum up the characteristics of all humanity. Until we become conscious of our interior workings, we experience these (and most) inner occurrences as exclusively subjective and through various emotional states that tend to *seize* us despite our best efforts.

The development of these two interior elements ("archetypal patterns," in Jungian jargon) begins with our emotional experience of our parents and continues throughout our lifetime. As we mature and attempt to leave the psychological environment of our parents, these elements lead us into life through the kinds of projections I have outlined.

Frequently, they flow into fundamental patterns that capture our emotional life, patterns that are infinitely varied and aren't exclusive in their scope. In one such pattern, we want our "other" to be a dream lover, who has the task of fulfilling our instinctual longings and the cosmic cycle imprinted upon our nature. We want this "other" to give us the love and understanding necessary to fulfill our psychological hunger, to gratify our desire for harmony, certainty, and pleasure. At each step along our way, when we figure out that this person will not do this for us, we become angry and resentful. Often, we think of leaving him or her to find someone "better suited" to us. But if we persist long enough in developing self-consciousness, we begin to realize this person cannot complete and satisfy us, for *no* other person can. We must mature and become an individual on our own, able to face or heal our psychological needs and hungers. Eros may point the way but it won't do our psychological work for us. This fact is tough to realize. Still harder is giving up the dream of finding someone, somewhere, whose presence will enable us to experience the fulfillment we long for. In a like manner, it would be a mistake to use this knowledge as a rationalization for staying in a destructive relationship.

Perhaps nature is destined to trick us, for if we go far enough, we always seem to find ourselves in a paradox. After years of struggling and persevering, personally and professionally, I have concluded that our attraction to the "other" may indeed connect us to our deeper self—not by gratifying our needs but by eventually forcing our search back into ourselves. Our hunger for harmony and certainty is often disguised hunger for meaning and creativity. If this is true, the *he* or *she*, by refusing to (or being unable to) satisfy our desires and remaining who he or she is, may indeed connect us to our deeper self, the container of the unerring path to meaning, authenticity, and vitality. Such "others" also force us to develop our own standpoint in life, including all the inner and outer work that enterprise entails. Our dream of loving and being loved is founded upon many confusing psychological images representing our emotional history and development. We must differentiate from these images in order to understand ourselves and avoid being victimized by our psychological heritage.

A second part of the fundamental pattern our projections follow involves our wanting our spouse or lover to fulfill these images in a sensitive, responsive manner—specifically, in many cases, in a way our parents didn't. We may want a spouse/lover to be totally understanding and an all-empowering emotional support in our life. Or we may want him or her to be unconditionally loving and accepting, bringing us sensuality, spontaneity, and happiness, whether or not we have actually learned these arts of living ourselves. Eventually, however, we must learn that the "other"—or even all of the "others"—cannot be our principal source of either affirmation or negation, unless we have abandoned our claim to personhood.

Our dream of love and the bitterness we experience at the loss of love seem to reflect our ache for a unitary reality, perhaps the one of which we have an intuitive remembrance before the exile that marked our birth, the exile from nature, the paradise of unconscious existence.

The projection of anima or animus qualities produces an intense bond of so-called "soul-mating" with the others. However, once we have claimed the "soul" part of ourselves, whether through time, fate, inner work, or because *the others* threw it back at us or refused to carry it any longer, we must understand that those others are in reality *themselves*. We must (provided they did not abuse us) treat them with dignity and respect rather than with bitterness because they "failed us." Paradoxically, they serve us as they force us to develop ourselves and our personal standpoint in life, and to re-direct into the transformational vessel of our interior the emotional energy we directed outward before. During this process of reclaiming projections, Jung suggested, men may need to "bottle" their anima moods at times; likewise, it is helpful for women to pour their frustrated animus energy into creative activities.

Some people may conclude that becoming an individual implies becoming isolated or too self-centered. Or it may suggest that we must no longer want love, respect, nourishment, and admiration from our relationships. Should we cast a skeptical eye toward our feelings of love? Not at all. Becoming an individual simply means we can no longer expect the people in our relationships to feed our emotional wolves, as we ought no longer to feed theirs. Eros and Psyche, in the ancient symbolic tale, are on an intertwined quest, his into manhood and hers into womanhood. Following concurrent maturing cycles, they are finally able to join in a relationship of two "others," seasoned enough through their individual struggles so their relationship may transcend their individual histories and lead to a life together that is fulfilled through the heart and mind as well as through the instincts. For this motivation to occur, they had to be forged in the fire of their own emotional development. Otherwise their attempt at relationship would have remained unconscious, based on illusions, and would have degenerated into a bitter power struggle. T.S. Eliot poetically restates the essence of this story for our age as he writes that the end of all our seeking is a state in which the fire and the rose are one.

The terms anima and animus are not meant to describe either states or literal concepts, though we who employ Jungian jargon often use them carelessly to describe emotional reactions. When a man is in a bad mood, we may say he is caught in his negative anima. Or if a woman is nagging and opinionated, we might say she is possessed by her negative animus. But these remarks are examples of labeling and oversimplification. The animus and anima are notions that express desire or its frustration at evolving levels rather than end goals of fulfillment or attainment. The man in a bad mood may be stuck in emotional conflicts he can't find a way out of. The woman, likewise, may feel powerless and unvalued, as much by her inner critical voice as by the actual people in her life.

If we are able to become aware of the effects of our anima and animus and can personify them (I have given two examples of dialoguing with my anima, my inner She) or provide them with some other kind of autonomy and creative form such as through painting, sculpting, or dancing, then they may also become our companions, enriching us with their stimulating presence. Even when fulfillment is attained, we find it to be momentary, because the flow of life carries us on to new levels of desire. Our nature never remains static, not even in fulfillment, and the function of the anima and animus is to connect us to this nature.

Eros, as a teacher, leads us to reflection and contemplation and to the poetics of life. Such progress and growth come from deep within ourselves and from our being passionately positioned in the river of life, secure in our own standpoint, like an island, waiting to see what life brings us. When we are in this reflective, centered position, the new often comes forth into completion in the womb of our interior.

Our times of gestation must be protected from the active, striving principle of logos, which is focused on getting things done. Instead we must use the strength of logos, the masculine principle, to protect our inner process and its territory. We need a lot of strength to safeguard this gestation process and make it sacred in a world that murders the inner life. In other words, consciously devoting effort, time, space, and attention to our gestations requires much active strength.

Through our struggles to come into relationship with our anima or animus, our masculine or feminine aspects, we can begin to realize a sense of inner wholeness that is grounded in the center of our being, the Self. But we must remember that this sense of wholeness depends upon our intentionally developing and maintaining a relationship with our inner life, our unconscious.

I am reminded of the words of the great Spanish religious philosopher Miguel de Unamuno in *The Tragic Sense of Life*: "May

God deny you peace, but grant you glory!" Eros, in a predestined and authoritative manner, invites and compels us into the glory of life, requiring courage, vitality, and inner and outer conflict. But, in addition, it does seem to bring us a reward in terms of peace. Life seems somehow to become more significant, and we find ourselves more grateful for it, trusting our belief in it to a greater extent, and living more happily. Paradoxically, our life seems bigger as it becomes simpler and more elemental.

Chapter 8

JOURNEY TO THE CENTER

Seeing Through

Earlier in this book, I said that when I was a child, I thought adulthood began with completing school, getting married, and finding a job. Then it lasted until death. But now that I'm older, this naïve view has been washed away, and nothing about life's journey seems simple.

As the second half of our life advances, we always seem to be traveling on a threshold, whether we realize it or not. This threshold divides the outer world from the inner. Gradually, if we are reflective, we begin to see the world *through* our senses rather than with them.

As a result of our progression, things that formerly appeared to be literal, concrete parts of a single exterior domain are now seen as parts of a twofold reality that has an interior domain as well. These two domains are separate but interact with each other. We learn that the journey we are on involves both domains, that it is interior as well as exterior. Occasionally, and perhaps to our considerable surprise we find ourselves falling through the exterior surface and plunging into the interior; or some *other* from the interior breaks through the surface of the outer, as if rising up, and seizes us. Self-realization expands the pattern of our experience with our own nature as we move through life. Once we begin a conscious relationship with our anima or animus, it becomes a guide that slowly and inexorably changes our journey across the surface to a spiral-patterned journey inward, toward the center.

As this awareness dawns on us, we begin to sense that all the elements of life are actually *within* us. The contents of our life are here, inside of us, before we live them and they are here after we live them. The same is true of life in general; its contents lie within us, though we seldom realize it. The child, the youth, the man, the woman, the old ones—everything that makes up a human being lies in our interior. But we do not have access to the entirety of our inner nature through our rational mind, through the one-eyed perspective. Access to our inner totality requires a second eye to be looking inward as the other eye looks outward. And the inward eye sees only through symbols. Because science, the dominant myth of our age, has thrust us all into a region of material, concrete reality, we need these symbols to connect our conscious self to the reality of our nature, the unconscious. Only in this manner can we see that we have a personal pattern to live that is embedded in the larger pattern of life. The symbols that connect these larger patterns to our everyday awareness flow from a source within us that is much older than our conscious mind, reaching us by way of our dreams and imagination.

The unconscious is not a simple dark abyss, for it is founded upon form, as all of nature is—elemental forms, the archetypes of the collective unconscious. The dominating, overarching form, the master blueprint in this structure is called the "Self" in Jungian psychology and is expressed symbolically to the linear eye as a mandala. "Mandala" is a Sanskrit word meaning a "circle formed about the fourfold nature of the square." Mandalas are depicted universally in religious art and are often subjects for contemplation or meditation. These meditations are intended to lead meditators progressively into a sense of unity and wholeness as they focus on the "center" and how their personal circle is nested within the universal circle of life.

The connecting symbol, like the anima and animus (which is often in symbolic form), acts as an additional bridge to our center.

Our inner teacher combines the theater of our sleep with scenarios of our imagination to produce conduits for a symbolic stream that both informs and supports us. The following example illustrates how one analysand saved her emotional life by escaping into a land of fantasies and how her dream-maker then helped her back into the fullness of life.

She had, to all appearances, a healthy, happy, and productive life. But this life that appeared so satisfactory was not her own in terms of the way she experienced herself. In order to survive a dreadful childhood, she learned to split her personality in two. To please her disturbed parents, she became a model child, a perfect student; she was obedient to the role they envisioned for her and terrified of their negative responses. She countered this submission by grounding herself in an inner world of fantasies. In that world, life became real for her.

By finding that island world within herself, she was able to be a survivor in an emotionally shipwrecked family. This split, however, continued well into the afternoon of her life. Her greatest happiness, her own secret, was to take long walks or drives alone, during which she had the chance to live vividly the fictional existence she had created in her imagination. The focus of our healing work together was for her to come into an experience of herself as a "person" in real life. As she was re-crossing this threshold, she had the following dream:

> I was standing on the balcony of an ancient building, looking out over gardens as far as I could see. They were shaped in many concentric circles. In the very center was a square made of plain earth. A man was leading a horse around in a circle within this square, exercising it. He was leading it clockwise, to the right. I knew the horse was mine. Slowly I walked through the gardens to the center. I was afraid he wouldn't let me have my horse. He looked at me, smiled, and said, "We've been waiting for you."

In the dream's circles and its square, we can see the formation of a mandala, the ancient archetypal symbol used as a focus of meditation to bring the scattered aspects of life together. The connecting symbol of the man—depicting a masculine aspect of her personality—is a link to her center, to her instinctual nature, which is now ready to carry her into life. Their symbolic movement from left to right, from unconscious to consciousness, emphasizes that her inner self is unifying her personality and moving her toward conscious living. It comes as no surprise that she awakened feeling comforted and secure, and that she had a sense of inner support for her life.

The symbolism of this dream dramatically depicts the urge of our interior life toward wholeness. Stories like this—of people and their dreams—leave me sitting in awe, convinced that some deep, unseen force from our center wants to reach through our lacerated selves, into our lost worlds, and heal us. It's a force bringing a great message of love.

Unthinking, one-eyed perspectives on these kinds of symbolic interpretations may lead us to fear that they are not "scientific." Yet Einstein saw through the physical world with his imagination, his fantasies or "thought experiments," and Pauli, another physicist, solved some of his scientific problems through dreams. Most of us know of similar occurrences and may have even had similar experiences ourselves. But we often find that trusting their genuineness is difficult because we have lost the ability to validate them. The truth, however, is that we must build our confidence in our own imagination, or else the information that comes into our life from unconventional or non-ordinary sources stagnates and dies. If that happens, the diminishment of our creativity, vitality, and personality soon follows. As I observed in Chapter 6, ancient man knew this fact instinctively. Before he learned to write, he illustrated archetypal forms standing behind the concrete forms he painted on cave walls during religious ceremonies.

Earlier, I also noted that while we are developing, we project parts of ourselves (usually parts we do not like or those from which we are disassociated) out into the world. Generally they stick on people who contain a little bit of the truth of what we have projected on them. Recognizing and reclaiming these aspects— parts of ourselves we have so naively tossed away—is a primary means for developing our total personality and a wider range of consciousness.

But if we fail to participate in life actively and personally, we will not have anyone close enough to us to awaken our projections. Then developing consciousness becomes a difficult proposition. Or in some cases, if others are simply too far away, our projections will turn bizarre, and we may find ourselves lost in a dark cosmos, unable to substantiate our reality. But if we are participating in life, then reflection on these matters can lead us to discover our projected patterns and to bring them home, where they can take their place in our conscious personality. Active participation in the world accompanied by contemplation of what we experience end up in a dance that fuels our conscious development. Often a little creative madness helps us keep both eyes open during this evolution.

These processes demonstrate that in order for us to truly have access to who we are, we must be actively engaged in relationships on many levels. Through our projections and our understanding of them, those other people will arouse within us an awareness of our authenticity and eventually evoke the whole person within us. As individuating eros leads us forth, we will progressively find that we cannot awaken that whole person without somehow getting in touch with the potential wholeness in others.

The expedition to the center compels a deeper journey into our humanness—and it isn't necessarily an easy one. An animal lives automatically, but the nature of Homo-duplex is not so simple. It requires that we consciously reflect and make choices on our journey inward, though the exact character of that task seems continually to elude us. Discovering the meaning of being human truly requires a careful, intentional journey into our center. Such is our nature though that, at least on the surface, we seem to be anxious and controlling even while desiring freedom. But once we are past the surface realms of our humanity, we find ourselves more curious, more attentively open to the unexpected, and more aware of the importance of being with others as well as the importance of being alone.

We do not have to travel far on our inward spiral to realize how distant from our true nature we have been. The closer we get to our center, the clearer our perception of reality becomes and we begin to recognize the interconnectedness of life—not life as an abstraction, but life as it is being lived through us. A feeling can develop, perhaps at first only a suspicion, that the underlying notions of the great religions may have some validity. To be deeply human is to be divine and to be divine is to *love*. Love has perennially been the binding force in life, recognized in the talks of the ages as well as in the lonely religious cells of the medieval alchemists as they searched for the symbolic gold in human nature.

Love puts us in the mood to risk everything, to give everything, and to dare an unforeseeable future. Desire, as an aspect of love, begins with instincts. As we mature and differentiate psychologically, our desire may evolve into the more spiritual aspects of consciousness and be reflected in aesthetic and cultural interests. Our desire becomes the foundation for passion, and passion means we care more for someone or something else than we do for ourselves. Energy flows through us and we are newly ignited and invigorated.

Desire, individuating eros, moves us along the archetypal path of transformation, supplying both the call to—and the energy that compels us toward—the future. Jung observed that nature itself is transformation and that it strives for union, for "the wedding feast followed by death and rebirth." Love eternally leads us through and contains us in this unfolding course of life, in both our inner and outer experiences.

Maturing into this stage of evolution gives us the impression of a reality beyond that of our youthful perspective. This impression comes to us slowly, through patience, and only as we develop greater consciousness. As our awareness expands, our relationships to the things in our life change and we enter a new phase of personal reality—seeing, hearing, and experiencing life in a new way. Joy joins despair in the cycle of our existence and the search (or need) for happiness recedes below the horizon behind us, for happiness is a morning concern. Seeking happiness as our only goal in the second half of life is regressive and results in our avoiding depth, avoiding the experience of joy and meaning.

In this new inner maturity, the child, the youth, the man, the woman, the old ones, and others are alive within us and we can be in relationship with them in our interior, allowing ourselves to experience life from many different perspectives.

Self-realization in the individuation process, in Jung's view, involves carrying on our biological identity—the task of *creation*—through the creation of our conscious personality. The passageway to greater consciousness leads through the various levels of life's bewildering paradoxes. As we slowly learn to appreciate the deeper complexities of life and reality, new dimensions emerge. For instance, we may be moved to take a look at the old image of Mars and discover that he is more than a simple god of war and conflict. He is a spirit of life and nature, vegetation as well, giving his name to the spring month of rebirth, March. Mars is also the lover of Venus, goddess of eros and life. His zodiac house is Taurus, which is associated with the month of plenty, and we are face-to-face with the duality of war and life, conflict, death, and new life.

The idea that the ancients were smarter than we have generally thought seems to be catching on. It makes a lot of sense today to look at the primitives and at the emphasis they usually gave to the second birth, the birth into self-responsible adulthood, during their initiation ceremonies. This ritual, like most of their rituals, provides us with a concrete example of the archetypal pattern of transformation and its manifestation at a major turning point in life. These turning points were unconsciously enacted in primitive cultures. In practice, however, the ritual was of immense help to the participants in terms of their learning that life was a matter of accepting their fate, carrying it through, and learning from it.

As this transformation takes place in us today, we must develop a personal context that helps us assimilate the events and experiences of our lives and thereby discover and become ever more fully ourselves. Such a new outlook may allow us to stop fighting life, to quit trying to "take control," and to develop a fresh attitude of participation toward life's adventures. The burden of fate is then carried with grace, losing its weighty aspect, and fate is seen as a pattern to be fulfilled.

For most of us, noontime is a threshold requiring a reversal of emphasis, from the development of form to the loosening of form, from looking out to looking in. We must remember, however, that developing form is a necessary task and those who have not done it—due to having been wounded or to other difficult circumstances—must find a way to complete it. Otherwise, they will sink deeper into their noontime distress—their midlife struggles. The woman who had the dream about the man leading the horse found, through her analysis, that before she could begin a journey into wholeness, she must come into the living world in her fully developed personality, not merely in a social identity.

This threshold of beginning, the late afternoon journey toward the center, may feel like a reversal. Or it may feel like we are arriving at and passing a horizon we have come upon unexpectedly. In any case, we ultimately realize we have reached a critical point. Where we thought we had come to know ourselves, we now realize we are struggling bit by bit to understand more and more about something that cannot be completely understood. Slowly we realize that we are struggling for a greater and more comprehensive version of ourselves for which we have no blueprint. The deeper we seek, though we do not fully understand what we are seeking or even why, the more we begin to realize that *something has found us.*

The Hidden Teacher

Early in our life, our indoctrination into the particular form of our society's education began. For decades thereafter, our focus was on the formalities of a one-sided mental and physical kind of development that ignored many dimensions of our nature.

The focus of our educational system is on the tangible and measurable, whether in schools or on the organized playing field. As a result, our development is skewed toward an orientation that constantly attempts to reduce a many-dimensioned reality into a single dimension.

Later in life, loosening our sense of form and looking into our interior allows us to notice something else, something unknown that has been at work in our lives. We see that beneath our "formal" orientation, our life has been orchestrated in another manner and that we learned many lessons of which we were not aware and that certainly we had not planned. Startled, we begin to understand a little more personally the meaning of St. Paul's statement, "It lives me." Gradually, the notion unfolds that the deeper guidance of our lives has not come from our everyday sense of "I" (our ego personality), but from some invisible center, a center that clearly understands truth as being greater than the so-called facts.

The young man Elihu, Job's counselor and critic, spoke briefly of a Teacher—a mediator, an angel—as he criticized conventional wisdom and the one-eyed perspective of Job and his so-called wise counselors. He pointed out that "God does not fit man's measure...God speaks in first one way and then in another, but no one notices...He speaks by dreams and visions that come in the night...Then there is an Angel by his side, a mediator, chosen out of thousands, to remind man where his duty lies."

Perhaps Elihu's Teacher is the one we have educated out of our minds. And perhaps we have been journeying toward a reconciliation with this Teacher as we have progressed through this book. Jung considered the inner teacher to be the Self, the elemental or archetypal form that stands for the unity made up of our full personhood and the pattern contained in the seed of our life. The Self contains the center and the circumference of our personality in an unmeasurable form, though it is a form validated by the experience of life, individually and, collectively, the world over. We find it reflected in the symbolic form of the mandala in most of the world's religions. To many it is the image of God, or the Divine within us, and connects each of us to the creative stream of life. Many views exist, in religious terms, with regard to the Self and what it means. My view is that it brings coherence and integrity to life's experiences and leads us to personal meaning. Learning to listen and pay attention to it provides guidance as we transcend our image of what we have learned to be.

Jung, sharing Elihu's point of view, noted further that there is "within each one of us another whom we do not know. He speaks to us in dreams and tells us how differently he sees us from how we see ourselves." Often when we think we have lost our way, the best thing for us to do is to pause and "see what the unconscious has to say."

An analysand with bitter memories of struggle and turbulence ranging from childhood into early adulthood had the following dream as he was crossing the threshold that, in his analytic work, would bring him toward the center. "I dreamed," he said, "that I was going before a tribunal for judgment. I have a strong feeling that I haven't measured up or satisfactorily completed the central task of my life. I am not frightened, but sad. I slowly realize that the group is not judging me. I am judging myself—my life."

I remained silent, listening intently. He continued, "Then a series of three transformations begins, each going to a deeper level. The first seems to involve the church. Many people are in golden ecclesiastical garb and the liturgy and music are majestic and beautiful. I kneel at the communion rail. I do not receive the host, but hands are laid on me and I feel electrified, altered, changed. I cannot tell if something is being added, removed, or both, or neither. But I feel transformed.

"The next level seems Egyptian. I am inside a huge rock edifice. There are carvings, incense and candlelight. Again, the scene is majestic and beautiful, but different from the church. Once more I am touched and electrified. I cry from the sheer beauty of the experience and I am overwhelmed with gratitude.

"The final level seems to be the most modern of all. As before, I seem to be involved in some transformative process, assisted by a host of people. There was no setting. No church. No décor."

As he finished, we sat in silence for a few moments. Softly, then, he went on. "As my eyes opened, I didn't want to wake up from the dream. I wanted to return, to stay in those places. When I got out of bed I felt refreshed. Even my body aches and arthritis pain were gone."

Once again, we sat in silence for a short period. Quietly he began to weep. I joined him, deeply touched by his experience—our experience.

A dream like this depicts the journey into wholeness—and its results. A life such as the one this man had led reflects the presence of a hidden teacher who, through the presentation of tormenting experiences, trained the man and thereby brought him to the capacity to complete his life's task. This task was to be a therapist—as, he realized, life intended him to be. The tasks at which he had failed taught him the lessons he needed in order to become a healer. Where he judged himself a miserable failure, he became charged with energy for vital work.

As a concrete, science-oriented society using a one-eyed perspective, we can document and triangulate such experiences, though we cannot understand or account for them. But as we move slowly toward and finally embrace a fuller and more mature psychological vision, we can identify with Faust, when he asked the spirits why they were here now and they replied, "We were always here but you didn't see us." There is a feeling of reunion, of being deeply loved, that is brought about by an experience of the inner teacher's presence, though the feeling is not sentimental or inane. It is a sensation of being at home in ourselves, and of renewed vitality.

Elihu further points out that God "…whispers in the ear of man, or may frighten him with fearful sights." Fearful dreams like the following one (to which I alluded in Chapter 1), bring people to my office more often than you might imagine. You may recall that a man dreamed his home was part of a Passover. The angel of death was to fly over and would spare all who had placed a note on their door explaining why they were living. Realizing too late that he had forgotten to put the note on the door, he ran out of his house, begging God for one more chance. A voice answered, "One more."

This man rightly became concerned upon realizing what the dream was telling him. Likewise, we must all recognize nature's imperative toward growth and follow it, or its energy will turn against us. Moreover, if we do not continue to grow, or if we begin to lose the psychological relationship we have developed with ourselves, we can become neurotic or even die prematurely. Thus, since the emergence of civilization, the tragic poets have reminded us relentlessly that living with a lack of conscious awareness compels a cataclysmic fate.

A new self, doing new things! It's often called being "self-actualized," which is a likable term. It carries the comfortable feeling that one has achieved a certain amount of healing and wholeness—inner peace. Despite all that, however, if we continue thinking in terms of the analogy that life is a journey illustrating the inner workings of the archetype of transformation, we must realize that we do not stop here—or anywhere—for long. Our sun continues to move through the sky. We get a clearer perspective when we acknowledge that our personality is always evolving, being born, living, dying, and being reborn again. This process is embraced when—in Jungian parlance—the Self, the image of God within, has replaced our ego as the center of our life.

The Hidden Healer

More than five decades ago, Dr. Jung[1] baffled a group of English medical doctors during a series of seminars they had invited him to present. The following exchange provides samples of their discussion:

1 C.G. Jung, *Collected Works* 18, *The Tavistock Lectures*, Bollingen Series XX, paragraph 382ff.

Question: "I think we can assume then, Professor Jung, that you regard the outbreak of a neurosis as an attempt at self-cure, as an attempt at compensation...?"

Jung: "Absolutely."

Question: "I understand, then, that the outbreak of a neurotic illness, from the point of view of a man's development, is something favorable?"

Jung: "That is so, and I am glad you bring up that idea. That is really my point of view...In many cases we have to say: 'Thank heaven he could make up his mind to be neurotic.' Neurosis is really an attempt at self cure... It is an attempt of the self-regulating psychic system to restore the balance, in no way different from the function of dreams—only rather more forceful and drastic."

I mention this discussion because, at a first glance, to conclude that something that is by definition unhealthy is actually an attempt to restore health may seem bizarre. In fact, the one-eyed perspective of traditional medicine, psychiatry, and psychology regards this with more bewilderment today than it did fifty years ago. Perhaps this has happened because the traditional approaches have become so entranced with methodology that they have forgotten the nature of illness and healing. But during these five-plus decades, many suffering people have pondered these thoughts of Jung and found in them an inner resonance that brought hope and changed their perspective from one of fearing breakdown and insanity to one of healing, transformation, and rebirth.

Jung viewed neurosis as a split, a disassociation from our nature, and our healing as a journey home to ourselves and our center. Love and war, eros and conflict, stimulate consciousness, and the personal quest is to bring these forces together in a manner that creates inner transformation rather than tragic outer consequences.

An examination of the above discussion with Jung makes it clear that, psychologically, our inner nature attempts to heal us through our suffering. However, our society's current psychological approach to human difficulties has become treatment-oriented and consists of diagnosing (classifying the "disease" on a superficial level that gives the illusion of understanding and control) and then applying techniques (that often show some success statistically but can rarely help individually). This non-personal approach dovetails with a tendency to *deny* the reality of inner conflicts and tensions. Both *treatment* and *denial* cause us to miss the voice of the inner healer—who is quietly and beautifully trying to restore us to a relationship with our healing center, the Self.

The Core of Life

The *center* has been the principal symbolic focus of emerging humanity, and it has been expressed not only in art but also in such forms as the design of living space, which was clearly shown in the configuration of primitive villages and early cities and towns.

The *center* is the focal point that stands for whatever is of enduring importance—the core, the meaning, or the hub around which life evolves. For archaic humanity, the creative mound represented the feminine principle, the womb of life and the center of the world. Later, as the masculine principle emerged, the mound was surrounded either by upright stones or an enduring central pillar, symbolically connecting earth and sky as the world's axis, ensuring the continuity of life.

A human personality, initially an ego, that cannot journey toward the center of its own being, the Self, is left unconnected, at the mercy of unconscious compulsions and motivations as well as social conventions. Paradoxically, however, these same drives may create the suffering that reflects our inner healer's efforts to get us into sufficient conflict to begin the voyage home.

An ancient legend speaks of the old Hebrew shepherd who, in speaking of his small village on the edge of the desert, remarked, "I am happy living here." Then he added, "But if I saw Jerusalem, I would not be happy anymore." His simple words are filled with a natural wisdom.

Jerusalem, Delphi, Mecca (the eternal cities), Mount Fuji (the central mountain), the Holy Land, and other numinous places have been considered symbolic centers of the sacred world. Ironically, many people among us live—metaphorically—in small villages far from their center, on the outer fringe of their personality, and seem quite happy there. Others of us seem chosen by life to be thrust into an inner journey. We become seekers.

Initially, we seek peace and happiness. But once we see Jerusalem, once we see through ourselves to the center, we cannot be happy again where we were. We see beyond the external, material destination we are likely to have been seeking and become aware that the pilgrimage is eternal—and inner. We may even feel alone in this crowded world, with only our inner Hidden One for a companion. However, if we can learn to continue, turning our (often reluctant and too rational and willful) focus inward to cooperate with this inner healer, then we begin our pilgrimage to completeness, to wholeness, toward feeling at home in ourselves and in the world.

The dream of a woman analysand lucidly brings the symbolism of the *center* and of our dilemma with busy lifestyles into a personal and psychological context.

> The setting was ancient Greece. I was standing in the center of a mound of dirt and rocks on a platform. There was a voice telling me some very important information, things that were not simply personally relevant but insightful, dreams and wisdom for all. The only way the voice could come through me was when my mind-body achieved a certain state of in-betweenness or balance. There was a certain point between activity and passivity, speaking and listening, that allowed the voice to speak. Many of the people in the area were not respectful and distracted me from my very important work. I was disgusted with these people because they couldn't or wouldn't hear the message.

Her dream reflects the problems of modern life, perhaps of life in any age. We must guard against letting the activities, the urgencies, and even the search for enjoyment in life, obscure the things that are most essential and important. We are challenged to bring into our experience whatever allows us to be congruent enough with ourselves to hear the messages of life.

The next dream illustrates the inner healer's use of symbols, especially the mandala and the *center*, to depict the healing process in another woman's personality. The story of her healing is revealed and illustrated in this production of the Self.

> I was walking outside, in another country, maybe Switzerland. I came upon an open area in which there were many people suffering. Some were autistic, some paralyzed, some were lepers, and some were disfigured. They were all begging for help.
>
> I wanted desperately to help them, but there were so many and they were coming at me all at once. I felt overwhelmed and helpless to do all the work that needed to be done.
>
> Then *the voice* told me what to do. I had to make an altar and place my four necklaces on it, along with my own teardrops. I also had to pull a hair from my head (my hair was long) and place it on the altar. Then I knew I had to lie down on my back with my legs spread out around the altar. Then I had to concentrate with my arms outstretched, connecting the lake and the mountains. I also had to align myself with the fourth ray of the sun.
>
> At the moment when it was all just right, the fourth ray of the sun turned into a lightning bolt and traveled through the necklaces, into my body, and out my fingertips to the lake and the mountain. This enabled all the hurt people to be healed. There was a huge celebration and I danced for them.

Beautifully, her Self used the symbolism of healing to permeate her being and bring her sense of unity, joy, and vitality—a sense that she *felt* as she awakened and realized she was moving into a new level of existence.

Unlike this woman, many people seem already to be in agreement with their world. Like the Hebrew shepherd, they are not urged toward an inner odyssey. They seem to be able to say, "I am happy here" or "I am content with my life." Others, who are not that way, begin the odyssey by searching for happiness and peace. Ultimately, they will discover that peace from the inner healer goes beyond the sentimental feeling of well-being and the absence of conflict. It represents the peace of persons unified within themselves and in relationship to their psychological center.

Shalom in Hebrew, or *salam* in Arabic, both originate from a word whose meaning approaches notions of being healthy, whole, and complete. In common usage, they may simply mean "good day." Or they may go a little farther, meaning "may you be well." From a spiritual standpoint "to be well" might have a deeper meaning, such as to have the physical and spiritual resources one needs. The word "peace" reflects a spiraling into the depths of our spiritual and psychological healing and development. Peace is also a word that draws us into the future, because it represents an elemental ideal that may always be realized in some way on a level beyond the one where we are.

Shalom

The perspective from which life is regarded as a journey urges us to consider the meaning of time. This perspective reflects an elemental pattern, one that is presented in the myth of Gilgamesh, the first great epic story of humanity, the theme of which carries through to the present. In this ancient story, which set the pattern for many stories that followed it, we find many of the elements I have discussed.

The themes of time and eternal life are its focus as it tells us about the Sumerian king, Gilgamesh. Early in his adult life, he encounters Enkidu, a wild man that the goddess had fashioned from clay. The relationship with Enkidu pictures the archetypal struggle we encounter between nature and culture. When Gilgamesh first becomes aware of Enkidu—part of his shadow that is personified by the wild, instinctual man—a struggle ensues until, by a combination of guile and strength, Gilgamesh subdues him. From that point on, Enkidu becomes a companion and supporter of Gilgamesh. Finally Enkidu loses his life, and this loss turns Gilgamesh from the concerns of his kingdom to the search for eternal life. Gilgamesh, in fact, also encountered several "feminine" turning points and ultimately was successful at gaining the flower of eternal life, only to lose it after a brief moment.

Gilgamesh returned home, matured and transformed by a life that had truly been lived—as life must be lived before anyone can know it, and as we must live it before we are capable of knowing ourselves.

We have talked of time with respect to ourselves—traveling back into our past with today's consciousness and then traveling forward with insight and with our companion, death. Such adventures, when we reflect upon them, enlighten us. We shift from the facts of our history to the meaning of the events that fostered the development of our inner nature. The resulting vision gives us a sense of time longer than the one we ordinarily think of as our own. It leads us to wonder how much of our story is the perennial *human* story, cycling inexorably through the stages of birth, childhood, adolescence, adulthood, old age, and death. It makes us wonder how much of *our* story is a story of *our times* and how we fit into these times. Similarly, in the midst of these wonderings, we must ask ourselves this: to what extent are our stories strictly our own? Yes, when we encounter the paradoxes of life we have the opportunity to make a personal choice. But by following the guidance of our inner teacher, our life becomes more than that, more than merely the singular expression of our individual story. For now it becomes nested in the greater story of creation.

As Gilgamesh wraps up his kingly duties, mourns the loss of his natural vigor, and begins the quest for eternal life, the story brings to mind the late afternoon period of life, the transition time from middle age to the beginning of old age. In the shifting light of the setting sun, forms change their appearance once again. The familiar landscapes of our inner and outer worlds change their hue, and friendly old landmarks may be hard to identify. Unfortunately, this transition has become even more complicated than it should be for us, because terms like "old age" seem to have lost their meaning as well as the respect that once was accorded them. But this time nevertheless represents another threshold, calling for reflection and consciousness.

In its entirety, our journey into wholeness requires that we attempt to unify the experiences of our life in order to apprehend them with a sense of wholeness. Otherwise, the present and the future may remain captives of our history, instead of our past providing the chrysalis from which we emerge into the future. This moment in our life is also a transitional time that calls for truth. As we begin to seek the center of ourselves, we are searching for the truth of our own conscious existence and we must struggle to understand the image we have of ourselves, the images others have of us, and the images arising from our depths—along with our slowly emerging understanding of reality.

The individuation process—consciously being in life in relationship to our greater Self—leads to a constantly evolving and deepening "I and thou" relationship with our center. Our greater Self (Self, master plan, image of God within, or whatever one prefers to call it) is an inner companion that teaches, heals, and centers our development. As we realize this presence and that it is the *One* guiding our particular strand into the web of life, the perspective we have on our life story changes dramatically.

Raised in the traditions of Western science, most of us think mankind has *evolved*, or struggled from a lower to a higher state of development. We hope to do the same in our personal development. If we have the time to study the classics, however, we find the perspective of the ancient Greeks to be just the opposite. Discovering that the forebears of Western culture thought humanity had *sunk* from an age of gold to an age of iron, from a time of grace to a period of barbarism, is a little startling. Conceivably, there may be a certain amount of validity to both views. Perhaps a wider vision is required if we are to find our place in the tapestry of life.

How then can we sum ourselves up as we approach the evening of life, the time when nature seems to demand yet another shift, one based on a coherent understanding of the many different dimensions we have experienced? As we seek to understand what summing up at this stage of life may entail, our listening to the following discussion may be helpful.

The man who had the dream of two shadows continued his inner analytic search and began his turn toward the center. He summed up the results of his previous work in two sessions we set aside for these reflections.

We planned this summary time several weeks in advance. We looked forward to it as a time to savor as well as a time to reflect, for we had both committed much energy to his inner work and shared the suffering and the excitement it involved. He began as we sat across from each other in my office, relaxed and anticipating our discussion.

"When I finished school, I poured all my energy, creativity, and craftsmanship into becoming a successful professional. As you know, I did this job very well, until I simply ran out of steam. I was overworked on one hand and bored on the other."

I knew he had left his firm at midlife in order to freelance and to be involved in a variety of ventures rather than to be so specialized.

"Somewhere along the line, in my late thirties, I guess," he continued, "I became restless. I didn't know it at the time but I was searching for connectedness, intimacy, a sense of being loved and at peace.

"My search took me to marriage counseling, and that helped a little. I tried an affair or two and, though exciting as distractions at first, they were soon more trouble than they were worth. For a while I got excited about men's groups, male friends, and male intimacy and I tried that route. I learned a lot from these experiences but they also left me feeling empty and restless after a while. Finally I came to see you."

I remembered his first visit very well and the paradox he was caught in. He was intelligent, sophisticated, successful, and well-read in psychology. He had been to many workshops and lectures and had tried several years of psychotherapy. In fact, he knew a lot about psychology, but it hadn't helped him. He doubted if seeing me would be any different and yet he hoped it would, because he now knew enough to realize he had been depressed for many years. Like so many other people, however, even some who are well-versed in Jungian studies, he did not know how to take his inner nature seriously—he was stuck in a constant process of trying to enlarge a one-eyed perspective. Following our peculiar American nature, he was continuing to do more and more of what was not working. In such a case, a massive defeat or breakdown seems necessary if we are to be able to stop and reorient ourselves.

"My approach to everything was heroic," he declared, "but in the unthinking sense of the word. What I mean is, I tried to get or do everything. Action was my orientation. I even tried to find love through taking action. And what I did wasn't always heroic or chivalrous in relationships. Often I was manipulative, wanting to be loved because I was nice or supportive."

"Yes," I said. "I understand." I had learned about the heroic and the manipulative approaches myself from similar experiences of my own, and I have seen the same pattern in the lives of many people.

He went on. "I have finally begun to realize that I am an odd mixture of things that God, my parents, friends, and my environment produced. If I can embrace this mixture, I can feel whole and unique. And I don't mean unique in the sense of being an extraordinary achiever. I mean that perhaps out of this mixture I can find a *moment in time* to feel connected, whole, and at peace. I suppose I could say that now my life flows better and I am enjoying ordinary things, probably for the first time in my life. But the real change I notice is that I no longer have to exaggerate and inflate my accomplishments to other people. I was shocked to discover the size of the illusion I had built up about myself over the years—in my own mind as well as in the minds of others."

I waited quietly, not wanting to interrupt, but aware of the elemental nature of his journey—one that I shared and one that, in some way or another, we all share.

"Before beginning my search for wholeness and peace, I spent over twenty years trying to prove to my parents that I was special and lovable," he said. "Of course, I also expected my wife or lovers to furnish me with that affirmation by making me feel special and lovable. It took me twenty years—and analysis—to build the foundation I needed to move into life."

"You were always seeking life, though. In one way or another, I think we all do that," I said. "We should appreciate our earlier achievements that help us become self-reliant. As you know, we need a foundation for going farther." I paused for a moment then asked, "What about your wife at this point?"

"I'm sorry for the battles we had," he answered. "I tried to make her play out my parental conflicts. But I don't feel guilty. She had her own part and her own baggage in our dance. I've gained a lot of respect for her and I guess only time will tell how we end up.

"Both of us now feel that conflict is really a creative dynamism that brings us face-to-face with ourselves and each other. Still, we seem to enjoy life more and we rarely fight. We have learned, at least for now, that relationships are not all love and nurturing, that they must stay grounded in honesty and transformation. Sometimes I enjoy my roles as husband, lover, father, and provider, and sometimes they are just duties.

"I remember the story you and I discussed," he continued. "I think it was from Barbara Hannah. Anyway, it was the one where, as life begins, we seem to get into a boat and start drifting downstream. All goes well until we hit some snags and rocks. Then we desperately find the oars, get them out, and row like hell back upstream until we are totally exhausted. Only then are we ready to learn both ways—to let the stream of life carry us and also steer with the oars, our consciousness."

I laughed—I who used to row hysterically at the slightest bump.

"The biggest lesson I've learned," he affirmed, "is to try and to catch a *moment in time* and then let it go. Whether it's a 'championship' moment, a moment in love, or simply a moment in the car with my son, I have to treasure it and let it go. I spent so much of my life thinking things should be that way all of the time that I became addicted to re-creating those moments. Then, of course, I lost everything except my resentment."

"Yes, I understand," I replied, realizing how much I admired his summation of our work. I felt that if he—or any of us—can come to such a perspective and to a relationship to our center, our later years can become the most meaningful and fruitful of our life.

As we said goodbye to each other, I wondered what we both would dream that night.

Chapter 9

JOURNEY TO THE EAST

Home

One of the deepest patterns in human nature is that of departure, return, and the journey implicit in between. I have used Jung's allegory of the sun traveling from sunrise to sunset as a framework for a psychological discussion of this departure and return, looking at our lifespan and at some of the crossings and voyages inherent in it.

Recalling our symbolic day leads us to understand that our morning journey is a quest for adulthood. Psychologically, I have presented it as a time for developing the *form* of our personality. The epic tales of humankind, symbolically chronicling this period of life, invite us to envision the birth of the world out of chaos, the dawning of light out of the dark void, and the power of a creative force bringing life into being. As these tales of our origins continue, giants are encountered, primeval monsters must be subdued, kingdoms are established and defended against barbarians. The tales are heroic, reminding us that we are split against ourselves and that creating our personality requires a heroic developmental effort and protection against the potentially unbridled aspects of our inner nature.

The second age of our development, that of mid-morning and early afternoon as I have presented it, may be considered a quest for life, during which we infuse our personality with vitality and the experience of establishing a life in the family of humanity. Such an enterprise furthers our identity as we grapple with how to be men and women—or, in other words, how to be adults in this family. During this quest we strive to further develop and finally to fulfill the form of our identity, only to find, as we pass the noon hour, that we must begin to release the strictures of that form. Often we find this journey doubling back on itself, returning us to the morning time, leaving us lost and wandering there until earlier wounds are healed, thus enabling us to re-establish our bearings.

This period lives immortally in the tales of adventurous developmental journeys typified by the tumultuous voyage of Odysseus; the travel downward into the cataclysmic depths by Orpheus in his search for the lost Euridice; the earlier search of Inanna, the Sumerian goddess, for her dark sister—all searches that still haunt us in our interior recesses. The later quests of Arthur and his knights, traveling alone into the dark medieval forests continue to call our attention to the elemental truth that we must persist in seeking life and that this adventure requires a lonely courage.

In the third age of our development, that of mid-afternoon, we find that our journeys and our odysseys bring us home again to a broader realization of who we are. We return home, to ourselves, with a knowledge of our mortality, as Gilgamesh did in humanity's first recorded epic tale, a tale in which his earthly brother Enkidu illustrated another pattern in our experience of living—the journey into the knowledge of sexuality.

We experience the symbolic elements in these stories as archetypal patterns in our unfolding life. We first fear love, though as we learn to love we learn to fear death and, we hope, go beyond our fear, finally relating to death as a companion. Like love, death threatens our existence by always beckoning us toward the far unknown, but our consenting to be consciously human allows death to become a friend, adding a salty flavor to life.

Each of these journeys revolves around great turning points in our life, some of which are organic in our being (like coming into adulthood, getting married, becoming old, and dying) while others seem to be born from the pattern of our particular destiny. Each, if fully lived, brings us to a new level of consciousness and a new perspective on life.

Returning home to ourselves and to a fully developed awareness of our mortality is what is symbolized by the journey into wholeness. The return home and the simultaneous loosening of the bonds of our provisional personality—the form we constructed to assure that we could function successfully in the world—prepares us for the next and, perhaps, the last turning point in our life. With direct knowledge of our inner Self and an awareness that life is greater than and goes beyond our transient personal identity, we are faced with the task of *living* our awareness, of actually giving up our ego-centered approach to life.

Few of us realize how dearly and deeply we want life to be as we think it should be, to respond to us and others as we would like it to—that is, in accordance with our own value system. Adamantly we resist recognizing these inclinations within us, these characteristics we summarize in terms of *egocentricity*. But this underlying structure in our personality must loosen its hold, allowing new consciousness and guidance from our center to be expressed through it. Thus, the constitution of our personality is transformed, as water might be when deep red wine is added to it. Egocentricity must be replaced by ego-*consciousness*, a growing awareness of our totality and of our place in the web of life.

The mythic stories of the ages depict the patterns of human life and how we experience them in terms of metaphors. If we take these metaphors literally or see them as historically factual tales reflecting undeveloped phases of our spirituality, we have simply robbed our inner life of its more comprehensive values. We serve ourselves better by bringing the moral perspectives and the meanings of these metaphors into our own lives and our own passages.

These ancient stories seem to declare symbolically that each life is a story of creation transforming into being and that each such transformation marks another step toward the essential nature of what we consider human. Our experience and consciousness are the thin edge of a new world, and our journey is one of ongoing discovery. These mythic tales of humanity give us access to the ac-cumulated traditions and wisdom of human experience, guiding us toward a realization that the story of the world is a story of love and a story of death, leading to eternal beginnings.

Within this context, Odysseus' passage is one that moves through the same waters as does our development today, haunted as we are by the interior forces of psyche and destiny. His adven-tures depict the beginnings of the Western intellectual tradition and the sufferings that life and our nature impose upon us all, upon the homeward-yearning human. In the anxious atmosphere of to-day, all of the psychological elements of the *Iliad* and the *Odyssey* are present in excess: the driving will to conquer and to achieve, both supported by technological ingenuity. Then, as now, in the rejection of the feminine and in the midst of violence, some deep, almost unheard voice echoes Odysseus' cry in silent desperation: "There is nothing worse for men than wandering." Yet, paradoxi-cally we are reminded by the Prince of Peace, "The birds have their nests and the foxes have their dens, but the son of man has no place to lay his head."

Once we have said yes to our odyssey and our humanity and returned home to our center, we find that we have traveled into self-realization. We have become conscious of the elements of our life, within and without, and conscious of our consciousness of them. Having found our center and come into relationship with it may even cause us to wonder if our journey is over. Some writers have suggested that Odysseus might give up his oar, planting it far inland where the sea is unknown, and stay home, tending the kingdom and living in mature balance. Others, such as Kazantzakis (in *The Odyssey: A Modern Sequel*), see that we may sail on until only the constant state of adventure has meaning—a process that led his Odysseus to a polarized and frozen death. This kind of fate awaits the person living life as a mercenary, who is addicted to adventure or who is trapped in the morning tasks of development and is never able to find or feel comfortable in the inner homeland. Herman Melville demonstrates a different attitude, as Captain

Ahab, ignoring the ancient Greek lessons of hubris, drives onward into a dark personal obsession against nature.

All of these stories possess a measure of wisdom, as they show us that when our odyssey is over, it must end—or we place our fate at risk. Psychologically, we must make another turn or we face the peril of Kazantzakis' Odysseus or Melville's Ahab, though this prospect does not necessarily mean we have found a place to lay our head.

Consciousness is a prize we must fight to gain, for the most part fighting against ourselves since we have an unfathomable predilection to resist it. As the idea of an inner teacher unfolds, we are led to realize that something within us has caused us to fight our longing for a non-demanding, unconscious life. An unconscious life may appear in many guises: demanding, unselfish, filled with accomplishments, flooded with busy activities. Often it may seem challenging and interesting, even self-actualized. Such a life may appear valid on the surface while, in fact, it is a suitably practical and apparently ethical excuse for avoiding a deeper call to meaning and the moral choices imposed by conscious awareness, as conscious awareness grows. Our inner teacher represents the urge for life and will lead us to seek understanding and meaning as naturally as the sunflower turns toward the sun—if we are willing to listen for even a little while. Our inner teacher represents a *knower* and a *seeker*, both speaking to us from within the guise of what we term the Self.

Our journey into wholeness, our seeking a personal relationship to the Self, enriches and enlarges our capacity for life. It brings us to a "seeing through" of our life, but not necessarily to happiness. Seeing through our life means to see through the practical, everyday realities in which we live into a world of Eternal Reality. Seeing through begins at noontime and, as our vision turns inward, we start to comprehend the world from which the creativity and vitality of life truly flow.

Early humanity reflected this world in the drawing and worship of elemental figures on the walls of caves—the great animal deities that they believed imaged the master forms of life. Evelyn Underhill, in her studies of Western mysticism, considers this world of master forms that nourish and inform life to be the world of Eternal Reality and Eternal Values. For the Jungian psychologist, this is the world of the archetypes in the collective unconscious, and this Reality is represented by the Self in each of us. It is expressed in form by the mandala and, in the Christian tradition, by the image of Christ.

Jung helped us delineate these dimensions of ourselves by referring to the part of himself that dealt with practical reality as his number-one personality, while considering that his number-two personality was grounded in the world of Eternal Reality. During the morning of life, our number-one personality gives us a stable foundation in the world (and "stable" may have many meanings). This foundation is necessary to support us until the time arrives that we turn our attention toward the ascending of our number-two personality, in the second half of our life. Connecting with our true center, which is within our number-two personality, clears our vision as we shift our attention to loosening the constrictions of our conventional form—the number-one personality. The creativity of nature and the archetypal pattern of the transformation continue to channel our growth, but the nature of our journey changes. It changes as the ambiance of an adventuresome odyssey that brought us into maturity becomes the ambiance of a pilgrimage, the journey beyond ourselves that is answering the call of some distant holy place.

In our odyssey, we struggle to become conscious where we were previously unconscious. The odyssey ends not with our becoming fully conscious but with our becoming *more* conscious—conscious of our death and conscious of our consciousness. That is: more fully human. As we had to become human, now the time of our pilgrimage arrives, when we must try to infuse our humanity with spirit and allow our life to manifest the transcendent values of the Eternal Realm—and we must be willing to accept this task in areas of our personality and life where we have previously been unwilling to be this conscious.

Perhaps we can envisage a fourth age in life, the late afternoon and evening time, as the age of pilgrimage. In many ways this pilgrimage is a journey into spirit, as Dante reflected in his stories. But since our structure itself holds the potential for our being spiritual, this pilgrimage is also a journey into the center of our own nature. If our personality is able to make this turn and our life becomes a conscious pilgrimage, we proceed farther in Jung's individuation process, and we also follow the pathway suggested in St. John's Gospel, for our eternal life now begins...in this life. In terms of the Jungian way of thinking, our pilgrimage develops as we strive toward wholeness and the completion of our personality, and not through some unthinking process of accumulating merit by doing good deeds, at least insofar as good deeds are defined by conventions and institutions.

Let us call this pilgrimage a *journey to the East*. From humanity's earliest times, the East has been seen as the fount of life, lying beyond the sunrise. The Garden of Eden, the shore of Noah, and the homeland of the Magi all lie beyond the East. The journey to the East thus represents a turning point in our process of development, as we reorient ourselves from a trip toward death to a pilgrimage toward the Eternal.

Reality

In our Western tradition, the mystical approach to God is intended to lead us into a dimension of being in which we all participate simply by existing, but become aware of only gradually, if ever. Living a conventional life implies living a life that is primarily unconscious. Such a life keeps us on the outer edge of Reality, never realizing life's supporting dimensions. The path of spiritual development parallels the course of the development of consciousness, and as both seem to be natural or elemental processes, they generally take us to the same or similar places, though they may articulate the process differently. Natural, however, does not mean easy, as we have observed that *natural* means conflict, life, death, and renewal. The difficult mystic way that Underhill outlines illustrates this fact, and a knowledge of psychological development under-scores it.

In the language of psychology, we talk about ultimate or el-emental forms, while in spiritual terms we may refer to ultimate values and reality. Considering how we might experience these two perspectives as having something in common may be helpful here. Perhaps, in the first, we are trying to know life through the mind, while in the second we are trying to know it through the heart. Jung, for example, insisted that we must give up our constant de-sire to figure out what we are going to *do* about something and to focus our full vitality on whether we *know* it or not—"knowing it" meaning to "see through" it. *Knowing it*, knowing the situation fully, means to have a carefully developed, comprehensive perspec-tive on it, one that includes such things as fully appreciating our emotional responses, recognizing our psychological part in the situ-ation, being aware of the response of our unconscious (for example, by listening to our dreams), and understanding how this situation is nested in the context of human development in general. Such a process leads beyond problem-solving to an enlarged and increased capacity for life. Thus, the difficulty that analysts generally face is in the form of this question from analysands: "What do I do?" This question, if allowed, reduces life to the objective level and to the seeking of self-mastery rather than healing and self-knowledge. The analyst is scaled down to an emotional mechanic and the notion of transformation is vanquished in favor of techniques.

"Know it"—that is, know the situation in its entirety—is a dif-ficult answer for an analysand to accept, or for any of us to accept, since most of us do not want to know it. We want out of it *without* knowing it. But this approach is nevertheless valid, for things that are unconscious change when they are *known*, and the foundations of our problems therefore change in the process. To get out of a situation or problem without "knowing it" simply invites its return in another, perhaps more drastic form.

Actually, the process of "relating to" a situation becomes integral to consciousness because we must be able to relate to the situation consciously in order to know it. In the psychological sense, relating to my experience means to separate enough of my ego-consciousness from it so I can observe, examine, and interact with the experience in my efforts to develop a perspective toward it. Job's behavior illustrates this process. He honored the emotional side of his experiences by tearing his clothes and wearing sackcloth. Consciously honoring the emotional aspects of an experience makes relating to it easier as we put forth our effort to know it. Then, further, he related to it with his counselors as they began to discuss, probe, analyze, and attempt to explain what was happening. They were trying to help him know his predicament through the mind by engaging it mentally, founding much of the discussion in their conventional frame of reference.

Let us consider another situation, one akin to Job's experience. Suppose a severely deformed child is born into a family. The child's presence may either destroy or sanctify the family. The same is true of dread diseases and other misfortunes. In such situations, we are faced with the question of whether we are willing to know them through the heart. If we are willing, and if we have sufficient conscious development (development that may be forced upon us by some of these very situations), then our experience of love and pain may refine us in a manner that opens our soul and transforms our affliction into a profound experience. If we know with the mind as well, we may discover that the meaning of the event is of particular importance in the story of our development.

One of today's pivotal problems involves our having institutionalized knowing—academic, religious, and scientific. These fields provide a dominant paradigm that circumscribes our capacity to know anything. Each originated in the human psyche and has an elemental core, with human experience gathered around it. We can propose, from the standpoint of Jungian psychology, that each of these areas represents not a search for truth, but a psychological complex. For example, science as a disciplined, methodological approach to understanding nature, is supported by centuries of tradition. Mythologically, this approach might be personified by the ancient Greek god Apollo and thought of as an effort to know life through certain aspects of the mind. Surround this way of knowing with the emphasis on the literal and the concrete that tended to support some aspects of science in the nineteenth and twentieth centuries and you may end up arguing about the truth of subjective experiences with those who fancy themselves scientific—who say, "Just give me the data. Back up what you are saying with hard data."

In such a case the person is speaking from a "scientific complex," not from a truly scientific position, which would be open to considering subjective experiences, including those of the imagination. "Science" as a field, or people identified with "scientific" persona, are vulnerable to being caught up in this complex. Such has been illustrated by the difficulty the field has with accepting more than one theory that explains phenomena or the tendency of scientific laws to change when passing from one generation of scientists to the next. Like science, most institutionalized ways of "knowing" develop similar complexes, reflecting their current perspectives.

Each of the above areas has been suspect at different times in history. All three have changed, and continue to change, our view of the world. Likewise, we redefine them in almost every generation. These domains have the potential to become perspectives in which we are trapped or dogma that dominates and limits our consciousness, as our current complex that emphasizes the concrete and the functional has done.

A utilitarian approach from any or all of the above fields might easily lead us to devalue the deformed child in the example we considered, even to the extent of believing that everyone would be better off if the child had not been born. Such an approach, however, is shallow and avoids a deeper knowing through both the mind and the heart. The idea is not to have a simple, practical answer, but to find a more comprehensive version of *knowing* what we are doing.

We think of normal or everyday consciousness as a type of sensate awareness that sorts out the essential features from the mass of experiences bombarding us. Once these features are sorted out, we try to set them into a certain order. However, this order will lack coherence and deeper meaning until our living experiences are related to the more profound Reality from which they issue and around a center that gives them wholeness. This is the more complex function of consciousness on a personal level—to bring life and values into an expression of realized meaning.

Our considerations of *reality* and *Reality* help us become aware of another pair of opposites that we encounter, those of time. *Chronos*, social time, is the time of ordinary life and also the time we use in our analogy that characterizes life as a journey from sunrise to sunset. But *Kairos*, the time of nature—and in religion, God's time—represents the eternal aspects of evolutionary time, here and beyond. Once we have gained a psychological awareness of our Self, each decision in our life requires that we make a choice between our personal preferences and going with nature's path toward completion. The very fact of realizing that we must make those decisions brings us into a living relationship with the eternal aspects of Kairos.

Such choices must reflect our more mature aspects and involve our continuing to retrieve discarded parts of ourselves, thereby increasing our congruence with the grand design of our inner teacher. Living in obedience to our inner voice rather than to a more traditional pattern will often offend those around us as we confront conventional patterns and what others expect of us. Giving up the "I want," the ego-centered and the conventional orientation, to follow the deeper path often creates resentments in others and, paradoxically, fosters accusations of selfishness. Frequently, the people who have been closest to us in our life will think the good things we have gained in our new maturity, or the love and spirit we have developed, represent a treasonable collaboration with Providence, meaning that we didn't earn our "rewards" the "right way"—by their standards!

Normal consciousness and our desire to have things be as we want them to be are usually reflected by those of us who insist on living within the bounds of socially acceptable illusions. Doing this, particularly if it involves deliberately ignoring or habitually failing to acknowledge what's plainly going on, is sometimes, in terms of the current jargon of addiction, characterized as "denial." In this case, however, I am not referring to denying the reality of substance abuse. Rather I am referring to denying the reality of an addiction to one's own will and egocentricity. Two particularly insidious forms of denial are "positive thinking gone wrong" and "accepting the unacceptable while calling it being philosophical."

First are the "positive thinkers" who always look for the best in things, always put on a positive face, and direct their focus toward getting on with life. Mothers and fathers who cultivate this attitude can produce several generations of psychologically wounded offspring by denying the nature of life and reality.

People who accept life too "philosophically" comprise a second group, one that appears socially enviable though it spreads a pool of emotional poison under the surface. "Our sex life isn't so good, but...we have a good marriage" or "...we have a good standard of living" or "...we are working too hard" are typical statements an analyst is likely to hear. These kinds of attitudes sound mature and understanding, even compassionate at times—on the surface. But life requires that we directly confront what we face each day. We need to question, analyze, examine, and encounter it as carefully as Job and his counselors did, seeking to penetrate what is going on, to know with the heart and the mind. By forcing a positive attitude or taking a "philosophical" stance, we avoid relating to our life and abort nature's efforts toward transformation. These approaches may appear to work but, in addition to fooling and wounding ourselves, we may just as likely be creating a wounded lineage that will continue for generations.

To live without conscious awareness and to be in such states of denial is to live irresponsibly and immorally, by denying the deeper aspects of ourselves and the deeper meanings of life. Of course, a life being lived this way may be hidden behind an impeccable persona in the conventional world. We develop these attitudes to maintain our social image and to avoid the very conflict and suffering we need to engender transformation. Neurotic pain flourishes in such people, often crippling them and perhaps damaging those whom they love, because—due either to fear or to conventional propriety or to both—they put a lid on their lives. (Freud and Jung clearly agreed that neurotic pain is a consequence of avoiding legitimate suffering.) My clinical experience shows that far more dysfunctional families and problem children are the products of parents who lead dishonest lives of denial than of those who are extremely physically abusive. People who live in these conditions of denial reduce evolutionary time to durational time, enduring life while living a charade, even though many of them often appear externally to be good and caring. Their living this way denies the transcendent aspects of life and, in Christian terms, renounces the entire meaning of Christ's message, which Jung regarded as a challenge to live *our* life, in the deeper senses, as truly as Christ lived his.

Our basic task from life's noontime onward is to be vitally engaged with living while loosening our attachments to the everyday world of activities. The mechanics of life are important but must not become so complicated that they absorb us. To remain engaged with everyday life without becoming either possessed by it or abandoning it is, in its own way, an emotional crucifixion that requires continual, intentional choices between values and activities for the sake of meaning.

Understanding the nature of time and reality as twofold helps us recognize and appreciate more fully our own twofold nature. Our everyday personality must live in one dimension, that of temporal reality, while our Self lives in another, the Eternal world. Both our everyday personality and our Self need awareness and energy and depend upon each other for development and fulfillment.

This conclusion leads to an easier understanding of the dynamics of transformational energy and their source in conflict. *We are conflict.* And the fire of emotion is what marks our conflict and is the chief source of our becoming conscious, of our bringing the light out of the darkness.

The "right thing to do" can seem very different from the viewpoint of what "I want or need," of social convention, and of the Self. The Self, however (and in a way unknown to us), is usually following a road much nearer to the desires of our heart and soul, one that often is also far from the desires and expectations of normal consciousness. But the Self can carry us from egocentricity to, as Tolstoy said, "Living for my soul and remembering God." If we live from this basis, our future, what we can be or do, is not limited by our past.

Once our pilgrimage has begun, our goal is no longer external achievement, though as our inner life unfolds and is expressed, it may dramatically affect what is transpiring in our outer world. Often, we may be charged with new energy and motivated to greater accomplishment. But we must be careful to protect our pilgrimage and not become sidetracked by issues of personal power and success. If we lose touch with our center and become too absorbed in cultural values that emphasize competition, success, productivity, self-sufficiency, individualism, or material progress, we may impede our ability to follow values for the sake of their deeper meaning. Then we may encounter a dark hubris and poison the fruit of our lives at its moment of ripening.

Pilgrimage

As we live our pilgrimage, we will find that dialoguing with the Self reassures us in the midst of our conflicts. Such a dialogue is highly personal and may be carried on through artistic expression, dreams, fantasies, active imagination, and other methods that maintain our relationship to our center. This process supports our efforts to build our life on an inner foundation. While religion may refer to these dialogues as "prayer," we will refer to them here as ego-Self dialogues. Their central requirement is our willingness to consciously accept our unconscious and its participation in how we live. In terms of a spiritual analogy, we are turning from a search for the historical Jesus to a search for "the way, the truth, and the life."

The dimensions we have been discussing—the twofold nature of time and the twofold nature of ourselves—are symbolized for many people by the image of Christ on the cross. In this image, the opened body (arms spread wide) of Christ nailed upon the cross joins four symbolic points of conflict or two pairs of opposites. One pair is imaged vertically and the other horizontally. The vertical represents the Eternal or spiritual dimension of the image and the horizontal represents the everyday aspects of life. The entire body of Christ joins these points in a manner that unites them through the body of humanity, connecting humanity to eternity and opening the heart to compassion. Symbolically, the cross also points to our emotional experience of being fixed between these dimensions. Repeatedly it exemplifies the moment of our encounter with the pain of transformation and of being human as we experience the conflicts of life. The arms, nailed open, strip the heart of protection, baring it and the full body to the world. The power of this symbolic image, when considered psychologically, is capable of transforming egocentricity to ego-consciousness and to the acceptance of the destiny of the Self. In the language of the heart, the love of power is transformed into the power to absorb life through love.

In this transformation, love has been cleansed by the fire of life and of suffering of its projective components and has entered the realm of eternal values, beyond our attractions, needs, and woundedness. From this point on, from the point of accepting the Self, our life belongs to the whole of humanity and is no longer completely our own. This turning point marks a further development of our capacity for compassion and love, values of the heart, as well as a revitalization of the feminine principle in our life. Compassion is the balancing force to creativity, which begins and matures through individuating eros and achievement in the service of life— and brings our creation, which is ourselves, into the service of life.

Another perspective[1] shows us that all three of the Eastern religions—Confucianism, Taoism, and Buddhism—agree on a simple

---

1   Barbara Hannah, *The Cat, Dog and Horse Lectures and the Beyond*, ed. D.L. Franz (Chicago: Chiron, 1992), 48.

point. They believe that the task of a lifetime is to bring all of our energy and talent into harmony by assembling them around a center that shapes them into a whole. The symbolic meaning of the crucifixion and the way of the cross extends the same message and includes the further dimensions of our emotional experience during the process. Psychologically, the image of Christ on the cross goes even farther, by symbolizing the necessary surrendering of ego control, the pain of this surrender, and the transformation from egocentricity to ego-consciousness. The importance of the ego in relationship to the Self and the effects on the world of its transformation are clearly depicted in this passionate symbol of transformation. Furthermore, all of the above religions (as do many others) confirm that this process is the necessary preparation for our journey to the East—to the Eternal.

Jung took humanity's abiding belief in a life *beyond* very seriously. The visionary side of humanity and our dreaming nature seem to characterize death as yet another transition point in life and not as an abrupt end.[2] In fact, if we are true to our nature and to the quest for wholeness, we *must* attempt to form a concept or an image of life after death, then search for the connection between how we live in our present reality and how we will live in eternity.

The individuation process is built upon the notion of our personal relationship to the transcendent and the eternal, to the image of the transcendent within us. It also follows the direction implicit in Christian theology and expressed in St. John's Gospel, that the life we live here anchors our life in the beyond. Countless dreams and expressions of the unconscious in people throughout the world accentuate this impression and the importance of our feeling a place in both realities. Such a feeling requires that we have fully

---

2   If you are interested in exploring analytical psychology and death further, two good books on this subject are Barbara Hannah's lecture on the "Beyond" in her book, *The Cat, Dog and Horse Lectures and the Beyond* (Chicago: Chiron, 1992) and Marie Louise Von Franz's *On Dreams and Death: A Jungian Interpretation*, trans. E.X. Kennedy and V. Brooks (Boston: Shambhala, 1987).

accepted the challenge from each part of our twofold nature and have attempted to live the tension between them.

Life, as I have noted, often sends us messages through the experiences of others. We analysts often find that an analysand brings in a dream, image, or experience at the perfect moment to crystallize some process of our own. Such an event happened once while I was working on this very chapter.

A man came into my office, a well-respected professor and author in his early sixties, whose childhood origins had compelled him into making a career of studying the interior life. He had been preparing a series of lectures comparing Jungian and Eastern thought, and he opened our session by saying he wanted to tell me about a recent dream, one that put a new light on his forthcoming lectures.

"I was walking into a large stone church," he began. "The blocks of stone were huge and covered with moss. It appeared very old. Slowly, I walked down the center aisle. Most of the church was cool, dark, and shadowy, feeling like a tomb. Then I noticed that the altar was surrounded by the flames of many candles. Each flame seemed to combine with the others until the altar appeared lit by the splendor of a single, central flame. As I was approaching the front, I saw rows of nuns in the old-style habits on the right and rows of monks in cassocks on the left. They were chanting with the deep power of an ancient Greek chorus—a power that can contain and channel the passionate and tragic moments of life."

He paused, then said, "I'm not Catholic, you know."

I nodded, remembering from his cue that the symbolic process is non-denominational, a fact that most people know but are surprised to discover when it is proven within themselves.

He continued, "I knelt and then entered the first row. I continued kneeling, head bowed. Slowly I raised my head and looked toward the altar. *She* was the priest preparing the Eucharist."

I knew who *she* was, for he had talked about her a great deal in former sessions. He had fallen in love with her around the age of fifteen, having loved her as only a shy, introverted boy could, totally lost in his feelings and never able to utter "I love you." They went steady for a while, as was the adolescent fashion in their time.

His shy, introverted intensity may have been appealing to her at first, but she soon left him for a more outgoing boy, a popular football player. He never blamed her for doing so and only regretted his inability to have said enough of the right words to persuade her to stay with him. However, his psyche kept her near and she remained an inner companion for decades, reflecting his ongoing emotional relationship to life. *She* was the one who, in his fantasies, he sought to, and did, impress with his triumphs, real and imagined.

She reflected his changing and evolving emotional states as well. When he was depressed in his mid-thirties, she showed up in his dreams—overweight, heavy, and disheveled. As he was going through a bitter divorce in his forties, she appeared in a series of dreams, crippled, wearing a full leg cast, moving about slowly and painfully on crutches. During a period of analysis in his late forties and early fifties, she seemed to fade away. Now, however, she had returned, perhaps to connect him to the transcendent or to his deeper self, as she had previously done with other aspects of his life.

"As the mass continued," he said, "*she* lifted the chalice into the air toward the large crucifix that was hanging from the ceiling. My eyes followed it upward to the crucifix. As I made out the features of the body on the cross, I found, with a shock of amazement, that I was looking directly into my own face."

A surge of emotion passed through both of us as he finished his narration. Moved to silence by the mood of the experience, I waited several moments before I asked, in a voice barely above a whisper, "What do you make of the dream?"

"It taught me something important," he replied slowly, searching for a deeper understanding of his experience as his features relaxed a little. "You're aware of the lectures on Jung and Eastern thought I've been preparing. I believed I had the parallel worked out. I was going to compare the ego with the *abamkara* and the Self with the *atman*, showing how they combine to make the *jivan*-person, and so on. I defined life, psychology, and religion as a very abstract, intellectual problem and then disposed of it rather neatly, I must say.

"Then I had this dream and now I feel very different. *She* has shattered an illusion I had about myself. Before, I saw this process—the material I was lecturing about—as universal and I thought I knew a lot. Now I see it as very personal. For the first time in my life I am beginning to understand the meaning of passion. This process is extremely personal; it is my crucifixion, my transformation, my Eucharist, myself in life in relationship to eternity—my death. When I awoke, I felt as if I had discovered some lost purpose in my life—one I didn't even realize was lost.

"From lecturing to living, you might say," he added, quietly laughing.

"You were still seeking something more," I added, "though you didn't know it. Something personal. And it came."

"Out of an ancient church," he said, "a church I don't even belong to. My kind of church, though, a church in the psyche—the soul."

Dreams like this one evoke intense feelings, even fear, because the strength of their images seems to go beyond the boundaries of our everyday imagination. But we shouldn't run from them. Such dreams are a gift, reminding us during our hours of sleep that every moment of our existence is a moment of personal meaning that, when understood, will lead us closer to the true gold, the imperishable meaning of our life. Such dreams, when they are faced with courage, reveal that living is not a matter of answering questions but of discovering questions, of knowing them and loving them.

Later, on the dark street walking to my car, I was still considering the experience of his being face-to-face with his crucified self. I contemplated how we all seem to have such a terrible time taking ourselves personally in a deeper or transcendent manner. We seem to have such difficulty overcoming our images of how things are, of how we are or should be, of how we want things to be. Yet we appear, nevertheless, to be in the hands of a Teacher who sends us lessons in the dark, through our relationships, diseases, and other experiences, to open us to the mysteries within ourselves and life.

In spite of our endless curriculums, we have little knowledge of what our Teacher has waiting for us. And the question still remains—whether we will value life enough to listen and to learn how to live from our center in a manner that acts to confirm creation rather than annul it. If we can value life this dearly, we can pass beyond the reach of ordinary time, as we do in intense moments of love, and discover that ancient path pointed to by most of the great religions and described in these words: "He who loses his life shall find it." The symbolic "Journey to the East" reminds each one of us that our personal life is repeating the miracle of transcending the void and nothingness.

Bibliography

Campbell, J. *Myths to Live By.* New York: Viking, 1972.

Campbell, J. (1973). *The Hero With a Thousand Faces.* Princeton: Bollingen Series.

de Castillejo, I.C. (1973). *Knowing Woman.* New York: Putnam.

Dunne, J.S. (1973). *Time and Myth.* Notre Dame: University of Notre Dame Press.

Edinger, E.F. (1972). *Ego and Archetype.* New York: Penguin.

Edinger, E.F. (1985). *Anatomy of the Psyche: Alchemical Symbolism in Psychotherapy.* La Salle: Open Court.

Eiseley, L. (1978). *The Star Thrower.* New York: Harcourt Brace Jovanovich.

Elliot, T.S. (1943). *Four Quartets.* New York: Harcourt Brace.

von Franz, M-L. (1980). *A Psychological Interpretation of The Golden Ass of Apuleius.* Irving, Texas: Spring.

von Franz, M-L. (1987). *On Dreams and Death: A Jungian Interpretation.* Trans. by E.X. Kennedy and V. Brooks. Boston: Shambhala.

von Franz, M-L. (1993). *On Dreams and Death.* Chicago: Chiron.

Hannah, B. *The Cat, Dog and Horse Lectures and the Beyond.* Edited by D.L. Franz. Chicago: Chiron, 1992.

Harding, M.E. (1965). *The I and the Not I: A Study in Developmental Consciousness.* Princeton: Bollingen Series.

Harding, M.E. (1973). *Psychic Energy.* Princeton: Bollingen Series.

Hesiod (1988). *Theogony Works and Days.* Trans. by M.L. West. New York: Oxford University Press.

Jung, C.G. *The Collected Works.* Trans. R.F.C. Hull. Ed. H. Read, M. Fordham, G. Adler, Wm. McGuire. Bollingen Series XX, Vols. 1–20. Princeton: Princeton University Press, and London: Routledge and Kegan Paul.

Jung, C.G. (1973). *Memories, Dreams and Reflections.* Ed. A. Jaffé. Trans. by Richard and Clara Winston. New York: Pantheon.

Kazantzakis, N. (1952). *Zorba the Greek.* Trans. C. Wildman. New York: Simon & Schuster.

Kazantzakis, N. (1958). *The Odyssey: A Modern Sequel.* Trans. by K. Friar. New York: Simon & Schuster.

Kazantzakis, N. (1960). *The Last Temptation of Christ.* Trans. P.A. Bien. New York: Simon & Schuster.

Keen, S. (1970). *To a Dancing God: Notes of a Spiritual Traveler.* New Preface 1990. San Francisco: Harper.

Keen, S. (1991). *Fire in the Belly: On Being a Man.* New York: Bantam.

Melville, H. (1952). *Moby Dick.* New York: Hendricks House.

Morford, M.P.O. and Lenardon, R.J. (1971). *Classical Mythology.* 3rd ed. New York: Logman.

Newmann, E. (1956). *Amor and Psyche: The Psychic Development of the Feminine.* Princeton: Bollingen Series.

Newmann, E. (1955). *The Great Mother: An Analysis of the Archetype.* Princeton: Bollingen Series.

Newmann, E. (1954). *The Origins and History of Consciousness.* Princeton: Bollingen Series.

Pagels, E. (1979). *The Gnostic Gospels.* New York: Random House.

Rilke, R.M. (1934). *Letters to a Young Poet.* Trans. by M.D. Herter. New York: Norton.

Serrano, M. (1966). *C.G. Jung and Herman Hesse: A Record of Two Friendships.* Trans. by F. MacShane. New York: Schocken.

Stein, M. (1983). *In Midlife: A Jungian Perspective.* Dallas: Spring.

Underhill, E. (1974). *Mysticism.* New York: Meridian Books.

Underhill, E. (1942). *Practical Mysticism.* Columbus: Ariel.

Van Der Post, L. (1991). *About Blady: A Pattern Out of Time*. New York: William Morrow.

Wickes, F. G. (1963). *The Inner World of Choice*. Boston: Sigo.

A Note of Thanks

Whether you received *The Journey Into Wholeness* as a gift, borrowed it from a friend or purchased it yourself, we're glad you read it. We think that Bud Harris is a refreshing, challenging and inspiring voice and we hope you will share this book and his thoughts with your family and friends. If you would like to learn more about Bud Harris, Ph.D. and his work, please visit: www.budharris.com or find him on Facebook: BudHarrisPhD.

Author's Bio

Bud Harris, PhD, as a Jungian analyst, writer, and lecturer, has dedicated his life to helping people grow through their challenges and life situations into becoming "the best versions of themselves." Bud originally became a businessman in the corporate world and then owned his own business. Though very successful, he began to search for a new version of himself and life when, at age 35, he became dissatisfied with his accomplishments in business and challenged by serious illness in his family. At this point, Bud returned to graduate school to become a psychotherapist. After earning his Ph.D. in psychology and practicing as a psychotherapist and psychologist, he experienced the call to further his growth and become a Jungian analyst. He then moved to Zurich, Switzerland where he trained for over five years and graduated from the C.G. Jung Institute. Bud is the author of fourteen informing and inspiring books. He writes and teaches with his wife, Jungian analyst, Massimilla Harris, Ph.D., and lectures widely. Bud and Massimilla both practice as Jungian analysts in Asheville, North Carolina. For more information about his practice and work, visit: www.budharris.com or find him on Facebook: BudHarrisPhD.

www.ingramcontent.com/pod-product-compliance
Lightning Source LLC
Chambersburg PA
CBHW021906020426
42334CB00013B/500